THE 21 MYTHS OF STREET LIFE

THE 21 MYTHS — OF — STREET LIFE

THE LIES I LIVED, THE TRUTHS I WAS FORCED TO LEARN

RUSSELL C. LATHOM

READICULOUS
PUBLISHING

COPYRIGHT © 2026 RUSSELL C. LATHOM
All rights reserved.

THE 21 MYTHS OF STREET LIFE
The Lies I Lived, the Truths I Was Forced to Learn

FIRST EDITION

ISBN	978-1-5445-5108-1	*Hardcover*
	978-1-5445-5107-4	*Paperback*
	978-1-5445-5109-8	*Ebook*
	978-1-5445-5110-4	*Audiobook*

CONTENTS

PREFACE 9
INTRODUCTION 15
1. STREET LIFE ONLY LEADS TO PRISON OR DEATH 23
2. ALL STREET AFFILIATES COME FROM ROUGH CHILDHOODS 31
3. STREET LIFE ALWAYS COMES FROM LOWER-CLASS ENVIRONMENTS 45
4. THE "G CODE" GOVERNS THE STREETS 55
5. CARRYING A GUN IS ESSENTIAL TO STREET LIFE 67
6. PEOPLE ONLY SNITCH OUT OF FEAR 77
7. STREET MONEY IS EASY MONEY 89
8. A PAID ATTORNEY IS ALWAYS BETTER 101
9. IT'S MORE GANGSTER TO GO FED THAN STATE 113
10. ONCE SOLID, ALWAYS SOLID 123
11. FAMILY IS ALWAYS LOYAL 133
12. THE HOOD IS YOUR FAMILY 141
13. GANGSTERS AIN'T GAY 149
14. STREET DUDES DON'T CRY 159
15. PEOPLE WHO LOOK STREET WILL BE STREET 167
16. REAL NIGGAS RUN THE STREETS 179
17. IF YOU RESPECT THE GAME, THE GAME WILL RESPECT YOU 187
18. YOU CAN'T BUY RESPECT 195
19. TRUST NO ONE 205
20. THERE ARE NO WAYS OUT OF STREET LIFE 213
21. FELONS CAN'T MAKE IT IN SOCIETY 221
CONCLUSION 233

PREFACE

I've experienced nearly every facet of street life—the grit in different cities, the risk across state lines, the worry in county jails, the adaptation in state and federal prisons, the criminal courtrooms, the faces of countless judges, the rise from nothing. I've lost it all, facing rejection from society, the betrayal of friends, the pain from the truth, and the comfort from the lies. I've won fights, gotten my ass beat, avoided fights out of fear, been shot at, shot others, been hunted by killers, and been snitched out, respected, disrespected, and much, much, much more. Unbeknownst to me at any of those times, I was conducting an investigation—observing, analyzing, and documenting my experiences like a reporter determined to tell this story, a story that morphed into a world beyond the world I knew, a world that has had many books written about it. But I stand to write this book, which has taken me a lifetime to write because it is the product of a lifetime—shaped by my circumstances, observations, and reflections. It is built on my emotions, experiences, and locked-away secrets and is crafted by a new outlook on patience, outside criticism, self-reflection, self-awareness, and self-control.

This is my lens, the truth, shaped by how I lived, remembered, and was ultimately transformed by street life, a world that existed long before I was born. For years, I tried to share these stories verbally, hoping that someone would hear me and ease the confusion I carried. But I found that writing them down gave me the clarity and space I needed. What began as a personal outlet evolved into a mission: to compile my experiences and extensive research into this collection of insights and takeaways.

The 21 Myths of Street Life is more than just a book about myths; it is an exploration of conversations often whispered but rarely voiced on a broader scale. It delves into lives—not only my own but also those of countless others—that have been affected by these myths and, in most cases, perpetuated them.

This book is as much about my personal journey as it is a critical reflection on the social constructs that tether so many to a life they never consciously chose. Through these pages, I aim to illuminate how I came to embrace what many call a life of crime—a path influenced by myths that shaped my decisions, my perspectives, and ultimately this work. My hope is that these chapters and stories not only resonate but also inspire reflection, dialogue, and change.

To make that possible, I write with two distinct voices throughout this book—but I assure you that both are mine. There's no facade, no pretending. As the streets would say, "no extras on it."

One voice speaks in the vernacular of the hood—a dialect shaped by survival, shared struggle, and an adapted culture that created its own slang, coded language, and expressions. This voice is raw and unfiltered, carrying the rhythm of the block, the weight of lived experience, and the mindset of someone who once believed the myths I now write about. You'll find this voice most clearly in the "Street View" sections, where I tell my own personal stories of growing up in street life—moments where I speak with *I*, as the man who lived it firsthand.

The other voice is more reflective and analytical. It comes from the part of me that grew through books, academics, research, prison libraries, conversations with others—in and out of street life—and a mind open to perspectives beyond my own. This voice carries a broader vocabulary and intentional thought—it examines patterns, breaks down myths, and connects street life to history, culture, and the larger systems that shape it. Through this voice, I discuss and explain street life in ways that may sound distant from the hustler or convict I once was. It may even appear detached from the street affiliate I used to be, but it is still me—just a different version, one that has stepped back from the smoke and can now see the fire more clearly. Somewhat like a doctor who eventually becomes a patient or a lawyer who may one day become a defendant, I have lived both sides of the experience, and both perspectives inform how I speak.

Together, these two voices are not in conflict but in conversation. One grounds the book in authenticity—the lived truth of the streets. The other expands that truth, challenging it, dissecting it, and pulling out lessons that stretch beyond my personal story. My goal is for you to not only hear about what I lived but also understand why it happened to me and to others, how the myths take hold, and what they mean for the bigger picture of life, power, and society.

These dual voices didn't just appear naturally—they were adopted out of necessity. Like learning a dialect or a new language in a foreign land, I had to learn to survive, evolve, adapt, and be comfortable in what appear to be two different worlds—two different understandings.

When these voices spoke outside of their assumed places of origin, one was seen as brute while the other was taken as arrogant.

That led me to a greater self-reflection. I began reading more, expanding my vocabulary, learning how words can carry multiple meanings, and understanding how easily confusion can spiral into hate and conflict, even when you think you are trying to avoid it.

I had an affinity for dialogue, human interactions, and the art of communication, which heightened my need to understand street life as I did.

This may seem like it was beautiful. But it was far from that. Trying to speak carefully, whether in or out of the streets, wasn't always welcomed—it could be met with pushback. Some people take offense when you are careful with your words. For some, intelligence without rage is a sign of passivity, while for others, intelligence without a degree is a sign of fraud or a facade. Your growth can stir up anger in others, as if it's a betrayal, and it can elicit hatred in the eyes of the academically educated who don't think you have the right to experience it.

But I learned that education, whether academic or self-directed, and language skills are never losses. In this book, you'll witness both voices working together—not to impress, but to express. Not to prove anything, but to deliver everything: greater clarity, deeper understanding, and a broader truth where need be.

My journey has been marked by the highs and lows of street life: victories and losses, love and betrayal, all of which morphed into a deeper spiritual exploration. This reflection forced me to examine not only my actions but also the societal systems and cultural narratives that encouraged them. At one point in my life, I defended these myths with my every breath—in many cases with anger and violence because they were the creed I lived by, an anthem that justified my choices, and a tool for survival in the so-called civil world, contradictory because of its hostility toward and alienation of even its own children.

These myths gave me a sense of purpose and a means to escape economic poverty, dysfunctional families, and social marginalization—yet they were also chains, holding me in a cycle I couldn't fully see. Even though they are myths, they are extraordinarily powerful, as all myths can be, so I must and shall respect their influence by giving each one its own chance to be heard.

For that reason, each myth in *The 21 Myths of Street Life* is carefully dissected and illuminated through deep analysis, research, historical events, and ultimately my own experiences, as well as those of both familiar and lesser-known figures who help bring each myth to life. To ground these myths in the world they come from, I've woven in quotes by street figures, cultural icons, historical men and women, and even government sources. These voices—ranging from J. Edgar Hoover to Larry Hoover, Solon to Stanley "Tookie" Williams, Maya Angelou to Cardi B, and many more—reflect the language, pain, culture, pride, and contradictions that shape the street mindset, offering a window into the psychology behind it and revealing why these myths continue to hold power over so many lives.

INTRODUCTION

There are three roads that stretch across the vast landscape of the United States of America: Wall Street, Main Street, and The Street—or, as some call it, The Streets. Each represents a cornerstone of the nation's identity, shaping its culture, economy, and ideals.

Wall Street, often called the lifeblood of America, fuels capitalism with relentless ambition and innovation. It is the country's most cherished child, its golden beacon for the world to admire. This street dazzles with its promises of wealth and power, projecting an image of order and sophistication. Yet beneath the surface lies a darker truth—Wall Street is also the birthplace of some of the most sophisticated financial crimes and is where the manipulation of wealth is both an art and a weapon. Once an exclusive domain of the elite, Wall Street has extended its reach, inviting the masses to participate with just the push of a button, making everyone's money part of its grand, risky experiment.

Main Street, the beating heart of the nation, is home to

the American worker. This is the street of labor, sweat, and grit—where dreams are built one shift at a time. But Main Street feels forgotten, its contributions taken for granted. It is America's middle child, plagued by "middle child syndrome," occasionally throwing tantrums in the form of protests and strikes, demanding the recognition and resources it deserves. It is a street defined by resilience, but also by a quiet yearning for more.

And then there is The Street, commonly known as Street Life, the veins of America. It is the last and least acknowledged of America's children—the stepchild, the orphan, the bastard that America perceives as a blemish on the nation's moral fabric. Yet it remains, pulsing through the country, like a runaway child, shaping and being shaped by its siblings. This street is hidden, shoved into prisons and marginalized neighborhoods, while its myths—romanticized, feared, or misunderstood—continue to thrive. These myths, passed down through generations and warped by outside perceptions, create a fog that obscures their true nature.

To those living it, the truth of street life is far more complex. It is a world where glamour is often a facade and survival comes at a steep cost. Yet its allure persists, captivating millions with promises of freedom, power, and raw authenticity. Even those from Wall Street and Main Street—the rich, the powerful, the "respectable"—find themselves quietly drawn to street life, sneaking in like visitors to a speakeasy, indulging in its forbidden allure, taboos, and profiteering, hoping to remain unseen as they cover their faces to run back to their own streets. Street life, the veins of America, carries the lifeblood of its sinful desires, its contradictions, its dirty secrets, and its unspoken truths.

Street life is more than a lifestyle—it's a multifaceted, evolving world shaped by survival, culture, and circumstance. For some, it represents rebellion against societal norms, a way to claim power, status, or autonomy in an environment that offers few traditional opportunities. For others, it's hell—an unforgiving cycle of poverty, violence, systemic neglect, and emotional exhaustion.

For those who live it daily, street life is often seen as a means to an end. It can provide a distorted path to success, a source of identity, or a space to build camaraderie and loyalty in ways that conventional society often fails to offer. Yet its meaning shifts with individual experience, geography, and cultural context. Some embrace it as a badge of honor, rooted in resilience, ingenuity, and grit. Others endure it as a constant battle, marked by danger, fleeting victories, and devastating losses.

Street life defies a single definition because it exists at the collision point between personal choice and external forces. It is shaped by poverty, broken institutions, systemic injustices, rebellion, ambition, greed, and a deep-seated human need to belong. For some, street life is a temporary phase—a game to play, a mask to wear, or an act of defiance in which risks are downplayed. For others, it becomes a lifelong reality—a code of "death before dishonor," the only world they know and wish to know.

At its core, street life is a force of nature—like dark matter, it pushes against the visible structures of law and order, adapting and thriving in environments designed to suppress it. It metastasizes with time, changing forms and names but always remaining present, a shadowy undercurrent that has existed before modern times and will persist until the end. And just as dark matter is understood only through its effects, street life is best understood through the myths it creates and sustains.

Myths are defined in multiple ways. The dictionary frames

them as traditional stories or widely held but false beliefs, often used to explain or justify something larger than the individual. But beyond this, myths are the stories people live by—ideas repeated so often that they take on the weight of truth. In street life, they function like unwritten laws: codes of survival, honor, and reputation, passed down and rarely questioned. They are part truth, part illusion, invented beliefs forced as fact—and they always carry consequences.

Through these myths, street life gains its power, shaping how people perceive it and how they live within it. This book unpacks twenty-one of the most pervasive myths about street life. These myths, from promises of easy wealth to misguided ideas of loyalty and respect, have shaped lives, decisions, and destinies. Beneath each myth lies a harsh reality—one that challenges assumptions and shatters illusions.

But this book is not an ode to street life. It does not aim to help anyone become a better criminal, nor does it glorify the chaos, bravado, and struggle that often define that world. Instead, it offers an unflinching look at raw, unfiltered reality. It's about peeling back layers of illusion to expose the deeper truths—truths that are rarely comfortable and often confrontational. Over time, the myths of street life have hardened into what feel like facts, repeated so often that they've been accepted as reality. As Nazi propaganda minister Joseph Goebbels once observed, "If you tell a lie big enough and keep repeating it, people will eventually come to believe it." These myths have become more than beliefs and truths for many—they've become identity and culture, reinforced by those within "the life" and romanticized by those outside of it. This book seeks to challenge those false foundations, dismantle the illusions, illuminate the darkness, and expose what's been buried beneath them for too long.

Writing this book was tough at times. Some truths were hard to face. But they remain, unyielding and necessary. This is not just a book about street life; it's a book about seeing things from angles that are either ignored or overlooked, with all their grit, gravity, and undeniable impacts, not only on lives within street life but on the lives of those who know of them, and even on society at large.

Many will reject these undeniable truths, clinging to the myths as a way to preserve something they hold dear. But as we will see throughout these writings, this book is grounded in the voices of those who have lived "the life," played pivotal roles in its cycles of destruction, and endured unimaginable experiences, making their words not only relevant but necessary to heed. This book is not just a collection of stories; it's a mirror reflecting the harsh realities too often ignored. Some may purchase it simply as a keepsake, a curiosity, or even a tool to validate their own beliefs. But I urge you to go deeper. Read it. Dissect it. Use it to spark conversation—especially in places where conflict, confusion, or chaos exist. Let it inspire change where cycles feel stuck and bring hope where it has faded or started to do so.

MY STORY

I was born in 1975 in Chicago, Illinois. By the time I was three years old, I had been brought to Compton, California—marking the beginning of a life constantly on the move. For the next fifteen years, I bounced between neighborhoods and cities so often that I lost count of them. This would mark me as what many would consider a transient child. Along the way, I was exposed to broken-down environments, dysfunction at home, police brutality, and more violence and crime than any child should have to witness, let alone endure. I was raised—conditioned—by the early wave of urban gang culture.

I was the youngest of my mother's six children—and the only one without a father. I had no blueprint of manhood, and no one outside of street life was offering to be a man I could follow. So I turned to the streets for direction, identity, some sense of love and belonging, and a means to guarantee my survival. By the age of nine, my first concept of manhood came from the behavior of fifteen- to eighteen-year-olds who screamed "Crip," "cuzz," "fuck the system," and "fuck the world" from the top of their lungs. I absorbed their ignorance, embraced their pain, adopted their code, and began to see life through their eyes. I was the blind being led by the blind.

Rebellion became second nature. I was a lost child. The streets fed me, clothed me, groomed me—and I believed they protected me. They welcomed me when no one else did. So I gave them my loyalty, and I believed that, in return, they gave me love. That conditioning was never easy to explain to anyone who had options outside of crime—family that they knew they could turn to if things weren't going their way. But for me, street life wasn't just a choice; it was a culture, a survival mechanism, even a religion. I embedded myself in its codes, convinced they would carry me through my worst confusion and pain.

But I was a fool. A lonely one. A naive one.

I didn't just flirt with the streets—I married them. I even had a kid with them, meaning I was willing to give eighteen years of my life or even more. And when my own children were born, street life and its codes still came first. I became an obedient lapdog, barking at anyone who wasn't—or didn't appear to be—street-affiliated. I thought I was defending myself, but in truth, I was also defending many of the myths I was taught, as well as others that were freely floating around in street life. I believed I was protecting something sacred, something real, something that gave me purpose. Pride. Brotherhood. I believed I even shared a mutual understanding with rivals—a code against a system I hated and a country I despised. I thought this code would push out the fakes and reinforce the pride of street life.

But pain and betrayal shattered that illusion. The people I trusted most let me down. Even my enemies, who I thought would at least honor the same rules, proved that the code was only real to me. I started to see street life for what it really was: a concept with no structure, no solid foundation, no one truth. Most people were just talking; it was noise. And that realization didn't set me free—it left me more lost than before. Hardened. Bitter. Barking at the wind. Tucking my tail when I felt alone. Shutting down when I was confused. I had no home, no compass, no true allies. I was a man on an island, and the more I experienced, the more pain I felt. So I dug for the truth, and the more I found, the more I learned, and the smaller my island got.

The world outside the streets was no better. Laws were filled with contradictions. Systems were hypocritical. People were greedy, deceptive, and full of pretense. Whether it was blue or red, Black or white, right or left, politics or poverty—there were lies on both sides. And I found myself caught in between, judged by both.

My experiences in jails and prisons only magnified those judgments. Still, the knowledge I had gained—through pain, struggle, and failure—meant something. Even if it meant nothing to anyone else. I began to gather every lesson I had ever learned, every mistake, every win, every loss. I collected truths and lies, opinions and facts, wisdom from people I admired and even from people I hated. I laid it all out. I wiped the slate clean and put everything under a new umbrella: humility. Patience. Reflection. Knowledge. Wisdom. Understanding.

I stopped fighting and rejecting answers that hurt my feelings or that didn't align with my beliefs. I let go of pride and began asking harder questions, not only from others but ultimately from myself. I gave myself time—moments, days, months, even years—to sit in solitude. Sometimes I retreated into deep seclusion. But in that isolation, I found the one thing no one could take from me: my lived experience. The things I'd seen. The whispers I'd heard. The changes I'd witnessed. And I found a new way to process it all.

That process led me to write this book. This book is about a life shaped by crime, pain, culture, and survival—a life that many will recognize. This book is not just about me, but about the people and experiences that molded a world of crime and molded me—directly or indirectly—through street life.

I dove into old and new histories, both in and out of the streets. I read philosophy—Eastern and Western, and even took college classes on it. I questioned the beliefs I had been raised on and the ones I had built for myself. I challenged my conscious and subconscious mind.

No matter how long it took, I felt compelled to write this book—not just to tell my story, but to bring voice to the many stories that lived, died, and still live on inside street life and the myths that surround it. As Michel de Montaigne once said, "I write to keep from going mad from the contradictions I find among mankind—and to work some of those contradictions out for myself." Writing became my way to confront those contradictions, to make sense of the chaos, and to share a truth often overlooked.

MYTH 1

STREET LIFE ONLY LEADS TO PRISON OR DEATH

> Street life only has two options: prison or death. This is inescapable. There is no other destiny that awaits those who play in a world that has no promise of hope. For better or worse, every story will end with the same outcome—you will end up behind bars or in an early grave, and when you sign up for the streets, you better know this.

Street life is often painted with a stark black-or-white brush: prison or death. While these outcomes are very real and should not be downplayed, the dangers and turmoil of street life are far more layered and complex than many imagine. The tragedies that emerge from this world often exceed our assumptions, revealing a reality that goes beyond mere incarceration or loss of life. As rapper Ice-T captured in his song "Colors"—describing himself as a psychopath and a walking nightmare—street figures sometimes embrace devilish or monstrous identities as proof of their fearlessness, often rushing to demonstrate it in action. In this light, prison or death may not even be the worst fate, but merely part of a darker reality.

For some, that reality is the torment of a lifetime filled with remorse, paranoia, and regret—burdens heavier than prison sentences or even death itself. Yet on the other hand, countless stories of resilience, transformation, and success challenge this fatalistic view. The same society that perpetuates the myth often contradicts itself by celebrating individuals who emerge from street life as self-proclaimed criminals turned legitimate business figures. But this transformation in some industries is often sold as a glamorous blueprint, especially through the entertainment industry—movies, social media, and of course, hip-hop culture, which at times glorifies drug dealing as a legitimate stepping stone to fame and fortune. As former drug kingpin and activist Freeway Rick Ross has pointed out, this narrative misleads young people into believing that street crimes are just part of the journey to mainstream success—while the real winners are the powerful media executives profiting from the cycle, not the youth caught in it.

These stories of survival and reinvention—boasted about in speeches, documentaries, and entertainment, applauded on public stages, and rewarded with financial success—send mixed messages. They reveal a truth many fail to acknowledge: street life does not always end in prison or death. Instead, it sometimes ends in fame, wealth, or admiration. Many public figures have shamelessly bragged about committing crimes to aid their success, while some have openly admitted to continuing such behavior—perpetuating an image of criminality that inspires those who view them as guides. As Cardi B once acknowledged in a viral video, hip-hop often makes room for artists to tell raw stories about their past, including the wrongs she admitted to doing to survive—such as drugging and robbing men. Her point is well taken. But when confessions like these are echoed beyond the music and out into the public domain without consequence, they blur the line between truth and promotion, reality and performance.

This contradiction cannot be ignored, especially when it comes to young people or ambitious individuals drawn to street life. For every cautionary tale about destruction, there are exceptions that inspire belief in the impossible. The myth of "prison or death" is thematic, not literal; it is often wielded as a scare tactic to deter participation in crime. However, these scare tactics have proven ineffective. When street life is glorified—immortalized in music, media, and even personal success stories—it becomes nearly impossible for people to be horrified by it.

Ambition has a tendency to override fear. When a person feels invincible, when they see more to gain and little to lose, prison or death becomes just another part of the cost—an acceptable price for an extraordinary dream. As Gandhi once asked, "What is imprisonment to the man that is fearless of death itself?" With this mindset, survival becomes more than a goal; it becomes a gamble, where even the worst consequences fail to extinguish hope. This makes the myth both seductive and dangerous, not because it is entirely false but because it tells only part of the story.

STREET VIEW

I grew up hearing that street life only ends one of two ways: in a casket or a cage. But from what I have seen, that's not the full story. While those outcomes were real and often repeated, many people beat the odds. They got out before they became another statistic—before their faces became printed in an obituary or captured in a mugshot. They quietly left the streets behind. No parade, no storytelling, just faded away. You won't hear about them because they're too humble to speak on it. The near-deaths. The near-captures. The close calls.

Some now have families, legal businesses, and thriving careers. They got in and got out, never allowing the hate, the fame, or the power to consume them. For many, it took one moment—a brush with death, a betrayal, a life-altering scare—to say, "No more." Some knew when to quit before it was too late. They "got the money and got on," as some would say. These people were not fake. Some were solidified, bona fide radicals. People who could still get vouched for by those deep in the game. Ask around and they'll tell you, "The person you see now ain't who they used to be." They took the hint before they took another hit that they couldn't recover from. They walked away with the stories but never repeated them, never glamorized or bragged about a life they survived, like many do today—even if they were proud of surviving it.

I know a few of them personally. Street dudes. Some were real gangsters. Others were real dope dealers. Pimps. Hustlers. Not the part-time type, but the full-fledged, all-day type who will never show up in a documentary, book, or rap lyric. Some endured cuts and bruises and gunshot wounds, but never prison. Some never even touched a jail cell. Though this is rare, it does happen.

Beyond those I know, there are countless others I don't—people who tapped into a brighter talent, accepted helping hands, took the opportunities offered, and built a new world that they call their own. They became thinkers, educators, actors, musicians, and poets. Maya Angelou—who herself once lived the street life as a prostitute and a pimp—once said, "I wrote about my experiences because I thought too many people tell young folks, 'I never did anything wrong.'" That kind of honesty proves that the myth crumbles when real growth enters the equation. Some didn't just dabble—they embodied a life of crime. Not for show, not because it was trendy, but because it was the only option they saw.

There are also worse outcomes. Tragedies of the heart, the mind, and the soul. Things that leave deeper scars.

Street life didn't sneak up on me or many others raised in places like Compton in the 1980s—for me, it walked through the front door of my tin can trailer home, sat at the dinner table, and made itself part of the family. It was a provocative lifestyle that eventually morphed into a culture. It wasn't just a phase, as some people thought. It became a curriculum: a *K* spray-painted next to a gang's name marked them as rivals—"killa"—while *RIP* followed by a name signified someone who had already fallen victim. For some of us, this was the syllabus of our education. "Street life only leads to prison or death" became just another slogan—one we heard so often that it lost its bark. Even McGruff the Crime Dog had no bite in our world. A cartoon in a war zone? Street life was real. And gangbangers became our role models.

We feared them. We idolized them. And we wanted to grow up to be them. That's why prison and death weren't warnings—for many of us, they were expectations.

Street life was a school of hard knocks. Murder was the subject, and your neighborhood was the academy.

Eventually, I started to believe that prison or death was something I could prepare for. At a very early age, I started to condition my mind to embrace it. And sadly, I did. I experienced prison. I stared death in the face many times, and it was talked about so much that it became normalized and I started to crave it—thinking that maybe it could be an escape from the problems I had and the pain I was enduring, or maybe it could answer all the unanswered questions I had about life.

But I learned something the myth doesn't tell you: the "death" part is never just about you. And prison isn't the worst thing that you can experience.

The streets never told us that tragedy takes many forms. When it strikes, especially when you're unprepared, it has the tendency to haunt you for the rest of your life. I've seen men lose their mothers or their children—some as young as five—because of retaliation. Brothers and sisters were gunned down simply for being related to someone affiliated. Some lost their entire families in a single moment.

There's the paralysis. The wheelchairs. The chairs you'll never walk away from. That's a kind of life sentence too. There are also those with challenges beyond the physical: a bullet struck them and they no longer know their own names. They have muscle stiffness in their arms and legs, and their eyes appear to stare off into space.

So no, not everyone dies or gets locked up—some are forced to live with what happened, leaving them bitter, tormented, and angry, which is often worse.

As for me, yes, I experienced prison. So in that sense, the myth became a truth. But my deepest losses weren't physical. The time behind bars wasn't what did me the most damage. It was the years of street life that took a toll on me. I lost my ability to trust in people and believe in something more than just surviving. I lost emotional connections. I lost aspects of my mental and emotional growth. I lost time—not just in a prison cell, but even on the streets—time I could've spent experiencing life, seeing the world, having more time to constructively influence my children. And because of that, I lost most of my fatherhood. Some things are inevitable, and some things are avoidable. But we must live with all things, no matter how we got there. No matter whose fault it may have been, I'm the only one who has to live with it.

The streets weren't a path I stumbled onto—they were a pavement I was placed upon. And if I learned anything, it's this: never use the myth as a scare tactic because we, including children, know that death is coming regardless of the life you choose. And prison—for many—can be avoided.

So no, street life doesn't only end in a casket or a cage. The possibilities—good and bad—are endless. Just be careful where you step because you can't step backward; you can't rewind time.

THE TRUTH

All choices lead to the unknown, and the outcomes of those choices—whether beneficial or not—will reveal their full impact in time. No one escapes the consequences of their decisions; even the innocent choices of a child eventually demand payment. Life is unscripted and often stranger than fiction, and its outcomes frequently carry unexpected surprises.

STREET LIFE COULD LEAD TO ANYTHING.

MYTH 2

ALL STREET AFFILIATES COME FROM ROUGH CHILDHOODS

> Street affiliates come from broken homes, absent fathers, and neglectful environments where survival overshadows innocence. Their childhoods are marked by poverty and abuse. They grow up too fast, forced into harsh realities, making street life an inevitable outcome. They are both victims of their environment and products of a system that failed them long before they could find another way.

The belief that all street dudes grew up with a rough life is as pervasive as it is misleading. While hardships are undeniably part of many urban narratives, this oversimplified myth fails to capture the diverse realities of those who navigate the streets. It relies on stereotypes that ignore the many individuals who weren't subjected to a hellish upbringing. In fact, some willingly allow these falsehoods to define their story without any intent to correct them—embracing the idea that they survived the harshest life imaginable. Many street affiliates exaggerate or fabricate aspects of their childhood, using a few painful moments to construct an image of relentless struggle. This kind of mythmaking becomes part of the initiation into street life, a twisted rite of passage used to justify certain behaviors or earn credibility.

In some circles, there's even a belief that if you're not aggressive, reckless, or entangled in the streets, you're somehow not "Black enough." Intelligence, discipline, or lawful behavior is seen as soft or suspect—when in reality, it takes far more strength to rise above the chaos, defend one's beliefs, and maintain a stable philosophy than to surrender to the unnecessary destruction. Even celebrities like Charles Barkley have spoken about how young Black men are pressured to believe that being smart or staying out of trouble makes them "less Black."

This destructive mentality can be found in all races, but street life since the early 1960s has been more commonly associated with inner-city Black and Hispanic people, even though white motorcycle gangs like the Hells Angels, the Outlaws, and many others were just as ruthless, and in many cases, much more deadly than Black or Hispanic gangs—not to mention white supremacy gangs like the Nazi Low Riders and skinheads. But television and other news outlets' constant display of harsh violence in minority communities has conditioned the public to believe that street life is predominantly isolated to "ghettos," while stigmatizing every child in those communities as having a rough childhood.

The "absent Black father" myth exacerbated this view of hardships in "the hood," and many children then, and still even today, associated the root cause of all their problems with their fathers. Even though this was an overhyped myth, marginalizing Black fathers as nothing more than mere "sperm donors" became another deadly arrow that pierced Black men's existence. This issue is addressed in an August 2020 article on House.gov, "The Truth About Black Fatherhood":

> In 1965, white sociologist and Assistant Secretary of Labor Daniel Patrick Moynihan published a report called "The Negro Family: The Case For National Action." This report claimed that increasing rates of "out of wedlock" births and single-mother homes among African-Americans signaled the coming destruction of Black families, and their trends were to blame for many of the issues facing the Black community in America. (The report has been roundly criticized by many race scholars.) Today, around 70% of Black children are born to parents who aren't married. (Rates of "out of wedlock" births have, of course, increased among all races since 1965.) The idea that racial disparities in education, employment, income, incarceration, and more can be blamed not on structural racism, but on this "absence" of black fathers has been parroted by pundits and politicians alike.

All the while, the majority of society began associating "good parenting" with single motherhood, attributing all the good parts of a child to the mother and all the anger and "bad things"—for the child and mother—solely to the father, or lack thereof. To craft the narrative of a "rough childhood" in the inner city, many children began to claim they had no father at all or downplayed his presence. Often, his sternness, efforts to assert authority, and work ethic were reframed as reasons to justify rebellion against him.

While rap songs like "Fight the Power" by Public Enemy were first intended to create awareness of disadvantaged Black communities and constant police brutality, other artists used their songs to brag about, embrace, or codify the many harsh realities of "the hood," and in many instances, these realities included having no father. Songs like "Fuck My Daddy" by WC and the Maad Circle, "Papa'z Song" by Tupac, and many others artfully expressed hatred for a father (or lack thereof) and that growing into success without him was possible. Dennis Graham, the rapper Drake's father, actually brought this to the forefront, rebutting the tales of him not being a father figure or simply not being in Drake's life. According to Graham, when he confronted Drake, he was told, "It sells records." And clearly, songs of hardships do sell. They also misdirect. Miseducate. Add stigmas. And hype an ungrateful mentality.

Early rap started to glorify these problems—everything from poverty and lack of education to so-called quick come-ups, or opportunities that allow someone to make money fast or offer an alternative way to rise to the top through unconventional means. Poverty-stricken inner-city children began to seem tougher and more resilient, like heroes, due to "surviving" their associated living conditions. They were credited with rising from the slums, "turning nothing into something."

Even suburban or middle-class children began to "play along" with the "rough childhood" concept, finding their way to the night streets, dismissing what many poverty-stricken kids would see as a blessing, and hoping to partake in a lifestyle of murder, mayhem, and horror, a world that demands so much and gives little to nothing back. Take the case of Michael Irvin, a Pro Football Hall of Fame star who raised his son in a gated community, surrounded by privilege and opportunity. Despite growing up far from the harsh realities of street life, Irvin's son began rapping under the name Tut Tarantino, crafting lyrics and tales of a life filled with guns, violence, and hardship. His father publicly called him out, labeling the persona a fraud, but this isn't an isolated case. Many who grow up in the hood also exaggerate or distort their experiences, using the street as a backdrop to gain credibility, attention, or status. This demonstrates that the allure of the streets can shape identity even for those who never lived its reality—further challenging the myth that all street affiliates experienced rough childhoods.

Not every street affiliate came from an abusive home. They weren't all neglected, starved for affection, homeless time and time again, or forced to sleep through countless nights of unbearable hunger. But there's a common assumption that a rough childhood must explain—or even excuse—"bad behavior." It's as if pain is used as a pass.

The truth is that many people—male or female—will trade the security of their future for the thrill or pressure of a single moment. They'll risk a stable home, the love of family, or the loyalty of a community willing to sacrifice for them for just one taste of what it means to stand on a corner or exist in an environment where hope and promise often get swallowed up. In these moments, many don't realize the transformation taking place. As author Kurt Vonnegut warned, "We are what we pretend to be, so we must be careful about what we pretend to be." The roles people take on—whether out of survival, pressure, or the illusion of power—can slowly become the truth they live by.

Consider the case of Patty Hearst, a nineteen-year-old white woman and heiress to the Hearst family fortune. In 1974, she was kidnapped by a radical leftist group, but not long after, she was seen on camera helping them rob banks and promoting their mission to overthrow the US government. Despite her claims of brainwashing and coercion, a jury found her guilty and sentenced her to seven years in prison. Her story, like so many others, reveals how adopting a role—whether by force or choice—can carry lifelong consequences. When performance becomes reality, it's not just the illusion that's dangerous—it's also how easily people start believing in it themselves.

The story of Lloyd Avery II is haunting. Avery played the trigger-happy gang member who murdered Ricky in John Singleton's iconic film *Boyz n the Hood*. In real life, Avery had no gang ties when he took the role—but after the cameras stopped rolling, the role never seemed to leave him. He began embracing the persona he'd portrayed on screen, eventually becoming entangled in the real-life streets he'd once only acted in. In 2001, Avery was convicted of double homicide and sentenced to life in prison. Just two years later, he was murdered—strangled to death by his cellmate at Pelican Bay State Prison, one of California's most notorious high-security facilities.

These stories expose the eerie truth behind the masks people wear: sometimes they become them. And once they do, the line between performance and reality fades, often with devastating consequences.

There are countless cases throughout history—and even more unfolding today—that mirror this same pattern of behavior. While many don't come from high-profile families like Patty Hearst, the underlying truth remains unchanged. People's need to belong, to feel part of something, is as natural as the changing seasons. For children, especially, it doesn't take much for society's built-in disparities to push them toward what is labeled "undesirable." Over time, those same children grow into adults and often repeat the cycle with their own children. The effects of this generational loop have been visible from the baby boomers to Gen Xers, through millennials and Gen Zers, and are now bleeding into the generations yet to be named. Yet this loop isn't fueled only by circumstance, but also by the myths that wrap themselves around these lives, disguising pain as pride and struggle as destiny.

This myth intersects with others, like "street life always comes from low-class environments" or "the hood is your family." But it deserves its own space because it reveals a different layer of truth. This isn't just about survival or poverty—it's about curiosity, rebellion, and identity. It speaks to the internal conflicts of kids who never voice what they're really going through—what lurks in the darkness that excites them, the forbidden worlds that call to them, the unspoken desires they can't explain, and the human need to simply belong.

It's the story of the "good kids" who "go bad," the ones who didn't fall through the cracks but chose to step out of line, who traded safety for risk—not because they had no family, but because they left theirs. They didn't want to be saved; they were seeking something else—a different code, a different tribe, a different sense of meaning—and in doing so, they found others who were chasing the same thing.

Ultimately, street life doesn't always originate in pain. Sometimes it comes from the hunger for acceptance, attention, power, or recognition. And when that hunger is fed by social glamour, music, the illusion of status, and the promise of standing out, the choice becomes easier to make—regardless of one's race, gender, or background.

STREET VIEW

As a child, when I looked around, especially at those of my age, I usually heard the sounds of anger or frustration. At times, I didn't understand the difference between genuine pain and the possibility that a spoiled kid was simply acting out.

Among many of us, a misconception developed that all street affiliates come from pain—childhoods filled with trauma, abusive homes, poverty, hopeless surroundings, absentee fathers, empty refrigerators, no love, no structure, no options. This was often spoken about and deeply believed. We assumed that this pain was what led them into street life.

This has become the default assumption, the go-to origin story for gangsters, hustlers, and "real ones" of all backgrounds.

Somewhere along the way, pain became the epicenter of the tale that many of us once lived or are living today. These are the stories we expect—and even require—to justify someone's involvement in the streets, their rebellion against society. Without that pain, their choices feel less valid, less understandable. So we search for it, assume it, and even, at times, glorify it.

But the truth, though rarely acknowledged, is that many street dudes don't fit that mold.

As I became more experienced in life and understood it from a broader perspective, I started to see that some of them came from homes where love was present, food was plentiful, and support was consistent. I grew up around people like this. Some had both parents; some had just one, but the love and sacrifice were there. Some lived in homes their families owned, rather than rented. Their parents worked—they had city jobs, government jobs, small businesses. Some even came from families with parents who worked in law enforcement. These weren't kids with "no options." They had options; they just didn't want them.

In fact, a few were proud of it, telling me, "I had good parents. I didn't grow up all messed up. I just chose the hood because that's what I wanted." Some would say, "I wasn't poor; y'all was. Nigga, we had shit." Another early childhood friend, who was one of my "crimeys," a person whom I would commit different sorts of crimes with, admitted that when he was growing up, he wanted for nothing. He wasn't starved for affection. All of his basic needs and beyond were met. But it was something about the thrill of robbery, the shock and pain he caused to his victims. No matter the crimes we did, being a jack boy—a robber—was something he couldn't shake. I once asked him, not from a place of jealousy but out of pure curiosity, "Why did you choose the streets? Why rob, hustle, and risk prison when you could just get help from yo family?" He looked me in the eyes, stern and without hesitation, and said, "Cause I don't want they shit, my nigga."

That right there told me everything. Some people weren't out there because they were struggling to survive. They were out there because they wanted to be, because the streets pulled them in. They were mesmerized, following in the footsteps of street legends. Rebellion felt freer than a certain type of responsibility, more exciting than routine. They, like many, didn't want the safety net their families offered: the properties their parents and grandparents owned and would eventually leave to them, the pensions, retirement funds, Social Security benefits, and more. They wanted the risk, the danger, and the edge that the streets presented.

Street life can be seductive. Trust me—I know. The so-called code of the streets gives people an identity—something that feels earned, dangerous, defiant, adult. Some kids weren't pushed into it. They ran toward it, with full force and nonstop, feeling invincible. They did so with so much energy they could've run through a brick wall.

Their identity wasn't born from poverty—it was born from defiance. Manifested out of curiosity or, in some cases, entitlement. They knew someone would always be there to bail them out, clean up the mess, and give them another chance. But people like me could only say, "It must be nice."

That quiet envy always struck me. Growing up, I was often the less-fortunate kid. Imagine that: being one of the poorest kids in a "poor neighborhood." At the schools I went to, in the neighborhoods I lived in, I knew struggles that many kids never had to know. And yet many of the kids doing the worst things came from homes and families some of us would have killed for.

I saw kids whose parents worried about them, provided for them, and protected them; who rushed to their rescue at every sign of trouble; and who gave them more than the basics—they gave them love, lessons, opportunities, material things. These parents worked hard to ensure or offer their kids a future, a better way. All the kids had to do was follow and accept the offers.

But for some kids, it wasn't enough.

When we hear that someone "had it all" and still chose the streets, it challenges the myth. So we start searching for a hidden trauma. We assume something had to be wrong—whatever we convince ourselves "wrong" is. We've been trained to believe that street life is always a reaction to pain, not a pursuit of thrill or power.

But sometimes it is. Sometimes it's about the rush. The lifestyle. The rebellion. The brotherhood. The attention. The danger. Being the toughest kid on the block. The ability to flip off society—and maybe even impress someone while doing it.

And once that myth—the broken-home narrative—gets reinforced through music, movies, and media, it becomes gospel. It becomes a "cool" story. The only story. So much so that kids who didn't struggle start pretending they did.

They'll say things like "I got it out the mud" or "I was born in the trenches," even if their parents were taking them to private school and putting lunch money in their pockets every morning. In a world where pain equals credibility, no one wants to admit they had it fairly good, someone gave them a helping hand, or their worst struggle was "taking on responsibilities." So they borrow someone else's pain and exaggerate their hardships. Because struggle brings status, sympathy, street validation.

But here's the thing: the streets don't care where you come from. They accept whoever walks through the door, rich or poor, loved or unloved, smart or confused. The block has one entry fee: willingness.

Still, people prefer their legends to "rise from the ashes," and this preference is embedded in how we see the world. Even Jesus—supposedly God himself—rose from betrayal, suffering, and even crucifixion. The Founding Fathers of America were not poor men but still found reason to chase power and plot a coup, all in the name of freedom and "independence." We want to believe that those who stand against the system, bringing it down—David battling Goliath—had no other choice. That pain makes their story righteous.

That's why, for decades, we've romanticized pain and glorified trauma, treating it as proof of authenticity. The deeper the pain, the "realer" the person. That's what myths do: they give us a script to follow, a shortcut to belief.

But in reality, not all street dudes were victims of hard times. Some were just reacting to themselves, wanting "independence and freedom." They had options. They had love. They just chose something else.

And many parents—good parents—never saw it coming. They thought their kids were just going through a phase. They thought the love and structure they gave would be enough to bring them back or keep them planted. But rebellion, once it finds an identity, doesn't always respond to reason.

I've seen both sides. For some, the streets weren't a choice. They ended up there because of conditioning and the pressure to survive. Their parents were dope fiends, alcoholics, selfish, or simply irresponsible, leaving their children few or no options. The fridge was empty. The bills weren't paid. The lights were off. The gas for the stove was turned off. All the adults had checked out or were on the brink of giving up, so the children either adapted or died.

Not everyone shares that story, but that doesn't make their stories less real. It just makes them different.

While we used to think a "well-off kid" couldn't be a gangster, reality proved that entirely wrong.

If you could get down—fight in any situation or shoot someone—most no longer cared how nice your house was. That pressure pushed some kids to act out even more. I've personally known a few who would use rage and violence against anyone they could to deflect the jokes and negative comments about them being the "rich kid" or "momma boy." Those labels categorize weakness, making many go harder than they needed to. For some, this creates an obsession with violence that leads to the solidifying of their names, washing away the stigma they did not want to be associated with.

I realized the myth was a lie.

Not every street dude comes from struggle. Some come from wealth. Some come from love. Some come from two-parent homes. And many come from opportunity.

And that's the saddest part—the potential they walked away from.

That's a truth we don't talk about enough.

But we should.

Because pain doesn't make you real. Poverty doesn't make you a gangster. And not every thug has a real sad story behind their chaos.

THE TRUTH

Street life is mesmerizing and alluring, offering promises of power, respect, and quick rewards that even a perfect childhood cannot guarantee. It thrives on the allure of adventure and danger, pulling people in regardless of their background or upbringing. While a rough childhood might make some more susceptible to its temptations, street life's appeal transcends background, proving that it is not always rooted in trauma but often in the universal desire for something more.

STREET AFFILIATES COME FROM ALL DIFFERENT BACKGROUNDS.

MYTH 3

STREET LIFE ALWAYS COMES FROM LOWER-CLASS ENVIRONMENTS

> Street life exists because of decaying neighborhoods, but its influence spreads to middle-class, suburban cul-de-sacs and upper-class communities, making them victims of the struggling lower-class environment. The ethics and survival mindset of the poor are an infection, seeping into otherwise "decent" communities—especially when these rough areas fail to contribute to the greater fabric of civil society.

Our society consistently places blame on inner-city communities—some labeled "lower class"—for the nation's social and economic problems. This myth perpetuates the belief that the challenges and behaviors associated with street life are exclusive to economically disadvantaged neighborhoods, commonly referred to as "the ghettos." However, the reality is far more complex: street life and its associated issues exist across all levels of society, manifesting differently in affluent suburbs, rural areas, and urban centers.

This phenomenon has long swept through so-called peaceful parts of America, challenging the narrative that crime and chaos are confined to and originate in poverty-stricken areas. Everything from white-collar crimes to serial killings, drug epidemics, and school shootings—all often rooted in or affecting middle- and upper-class America—can be traced to elements deeply connected to street life. While many see the "lower class" as animals, when crime happens in their own communities, they say, "I can't believe this is happening here," but they do not stigmatize the perpetrators in the same way.

Yet America has a longstanding tendency to sidestep responsibility for the very dysfunctions it has helped create. Rather than facing the consequences of policies shaped by greed, discrimination, and systemic neglect, laying the blame at the feet of the poor becomes far more convenient. Those in power often shape the narrative in their favor, rewriting history to mask their own role in the damage it has caused. As economist Jeffrey Sachs once pointed out, when the wealthy control the story, the poor end up taking the fall for everything. This blame game doesn't just distort the truth—it protects the systems that continue to cause harm.

For example, in 1994, Senator Joe Biden, who would later become president, authored the Violent Crime Control and Law Enforcement Act, commonly known as the Crime Bill. This legislation contributed to mass incarceration, disproportionately impacting Black and Brown communities, families, and fatherhood by increasing prison sentences and expanding the scope of criminal charges. Nearly three decades later, his son, Hunter Biden, faced federal charges, including lying about his drug use on a firearm purchase form and failing to file and pay taxes. Before serving any time, Hunter received a pardon from Joe Biden, highlighting a stark contrast between the harsh consequences of the Crime Bill for many Americans and the leniency extended within the system—a situation some view as emblematic of systemic inequities in justice. Although Biden later commuted many sentences and pardoned some before leaving the presidency, this doesn't change the reality of the thirty years of damage caused by the bill that he wrote and that Congress—including many Black leaders—signed on to.

To expand on this point, consider Purdue Pharma, a pharmaceutical company once controlled by the wealthy and influential Sackler family. Purdue developed and aggressively marketed the opioid painkiller OxyContin, falsely claiming it was less addictive than other opioids. Internal documents and investigations later revealed that the company knew of the drug's highly addictive properties but continued pushing it anyway. Their relentless promotion contributed directly to the opioid epidemic, which has killed over 500,000 people in the US alone.

Despite the catastrophic consequences of their actions, not a single member of the Sackler family went to prison. Purdue Pharma faced fines and civil settlements totaling billions, but before the company declared bankruptcy, the Sacklers were allowed to keep much of their personal fortune—shielded by legal maneuvering and a system that often protects the wealthy from full accountability.

But when someone from a housing project sells even a fraction of what the Sacklers distributed—whether it be crack, heroin, or counterfeit pills—they get decades in prison, or worse. The only real differences are class, appearance, connections, and race. The same hustle that gets glorified or criminalized in the streets is repackaged as "business" when it's happening in boardrooms. As Solon, an Athenian once noted, Justice isn't real until the unaffected cares as much as the oppressed.

This perspective demonstrates that "street life"—defined by manipulation, profit from addiction, and disregard for human consequences—doesn't just come from the bottom. It's replicated in corporate offices, political corridors, and elite families with far more reach and protection. What changes is not the behavior, but how society labels and responds to it. Street life is not about where you come from—it's about what you're willing to do for power, control, and money, no matter the cost.

That's why tying street life exclusively to one class is misleading. As we know, the US is divided into class systems—lower, middle, and upper classes—often determined by financial means. Street life is frequently imagined as a product of poor living conditions and is therefore associated with the "lower class." But this perception is far from the truth. Criminal behavior and street culture, as we can clearly see, transcend class boundaries. Communities of all income levels have produced individuals involved in criminal activities, from petty theft to large-scale organized crime, often driven by greed, power, economic desperation, cultural influences, or sheer ambition.

"Where justice is denied, where poverty is enforced, where ignorance prevails, and where one class is made to feel that society is an organized conspiracy to oppress, rob, and degrade them, neither persons nor property will be safe."

—FREDERICK DOUGLASS

Middle-class households—typically defined as earning between two-thirds and twice the median US income—often find themselves straddling different social and economic environments. Some choose to live in traditionally lower-income neighborhoods to save money or get a better deal on housing, while others stretch their budgets to reside in more affluent areas, hoping to project success or offer their families better opportunities. This behavior reflects what's long been called "keeping up with the Joneses"—a phrase that predates today's *Keeping Up with the Kardashians* but conveys a similar meaning: the desire to match or surpass the lifestyle of those perceived to have more. In doing so, many willingly fall into debt, chasing an image of success that may be more about appearance than reality.

But regardless of geography, middle-class and upper-class children are not immune to the allure of street life. Despite access to better opportunities, many are drawn to its promise of rebellion, freedom, and power—values often glamorized in entertainment and pop culture. Parents frequently ask, "How could this happen, when we've worked so hard to provide for our children?" Ironically, the privileges they provide may inadvertently contribute to the problem by shielding children from the realities of hard work, delayed gratification, and early knowledge or teachings about what they assume is attractive.

Additionally, young people—like adults—crave a sense of belonging and independence. Street life offers them the illusion of both. It represents rebellion against authority, self-determination, and a chance to be part of something larger than themselves. To many, it projects strength, wealth, and glory—the very markers of success that society holds in high regard. When parents overlook these influences or even directly or indirectly introduce their children to them, young people may become consumed by the allure of street culture, often falling victim to its harsh realities.

A public service announcement, often broadcast on American television from the 1960s to the 1980s, asked, "Do you know where your kids are?" It was a question posed in 1961 by a state senator who urged broadcasters to ask the question on air to remind parents to check in with their children. The concern behind that question still echoes today—as a warning not just about physical whereabouts, but about emotional and moral direction.

Because while we as parents may know where our children are geographically, especially with technology like GPS built into our phones, we might not realize where their minds and identities are drifting. Street life, as an entity, transcends boundaries and defies stereotypes. It does not discriminate by race, gender, or socioeconomic status. Its message is both alluring and foreboding: the doors are open to all who are willing to enter, but the costs often outweigh the rewards. It exists as a subculture within society, a shadow that thrives on society's neglect and fractures. While many of us fail to acknowledge the interconnectedness of communities within a society, it is an undeniable truth that when one part begins to falter, the effects ripple outward, destabilizing the whole.

Yet instead of addressing these cracks collectively, we are often blinded by competitive greed, cultural divides, deep-seated racial prejudices, and the need to control and subdue others. These forces erode the foundation of loving and civil behavior, fueling mistrust and widening the gap between communities. Street culture thrives in these divides, feeding off the disconnection and neglect that allow it to grow unchecked. It is both a symptom and a consequence of society's failure to see itself as a collective whole, bound together by shared responsibility.

STREET VIEW

My childhood was unstable—physically, mentally, and emotionally. I was a transient child, moving at least once a year from city to city, neighborhood to neighborhood. At the time, I didn't fully grasp what stability meant or how necessary it was. But through all that trauma, I worked hard to give myself the ability to see people, neighborhoods, and the streets from a broader perspective. Sometimes the communities I landed in didn't look "ghetto," but even in those quiet corners, street life existed. It didn't always look like the movies or the places I came from, but it was there just the same.

The myth that street life is born only in the "ghettos" or low-income neighborhoods is a narrow, misguided view of a much more complex reality. It's easy to associate street life with poverty—crumbling buildings, corner hustlers, liquor stores, and generational struggle—but when I was growing up, the streets didn't care about your zip code. They didn't ask where you came from. They asked for your mind, your pain, your loyalty, your attention, your identity—and every day, they begged for your life.

I saw this myth unravel firsthand. I briefly lived in neighborhoods that looked like something out of *The Cosby Show*—clean streets, polite neighbors, nice homes—and yet, beneath that polished surface was the same street mentality I saw in the worst parts of the hood. Gangbangers of all races. Middle-class kids eager to "earn their stripes" as street soldiers—blue rags, red rags, baggy clothes hiding guns as if their neighborhood was a war zone. As a kid, I couldn't understand it. Why would someone with all of this—dedicated, hardworking parents, front lawns with nicely cut grass, and sometimes a backyard swimming pool—want to be in the streets? Didn't they have enough? Isn't this what kids like me begged for? Isn't this what a life of crime is supposed to bring?

The truth is that street life has many doorways, and you don't always have to knock. These weren't some poor kids looking for a way out. These were middle-class kids wanting a way into something—to belong, to be feared, to feel alive.

As I got older, I saw street life take on new faces. It wasn't just hood politics and "trap houses" anymore. I saw it behind computer screens, friends taking the hood into the military, into college lecture halls. Some street affiliates spoke street slang. Some spoke corporate. Some rode Harleys. Others drove Bentleys. Pick your poison. Street life doesn't always come with boarded-up windows and corner-store shootouts. Sometimes it wears a Rolex and grills you about stocks over dinner.

My own rise in the streets showed me this firsthand. With more money and a bigger operation came deeper connections—and bigger targets. Some of my suppliers didn't live in the neighborhoods I came from. They lived in quiet, upscale communities with perfect lawns and smiling, waving neighbors. They had real careers, big families, and old money. Sometimes while we ate dinner in their beautiful homes, my car was being packed with drugs in their garage. I'd drive away through neighborhoods so quiet they scared me. I feared being racially profiled before I even made it to the freeway. Truth be told, I was more afraid of their neighbors than their neighbors were probably afraid of me.

Some of my "connects" looked like high school kids—driving nicer cars than their parents'. I met dealers from blue-collar backgrounds and white-collar privilege. They didn't all speak street. Some of them barely spoke English. Some didn't even have a tattoo. But they had no limits on the crimes they were willing to commit.

That's when I realized—there are cocaine dealers in cul-de-sacs. Meth pushers in the mountains. Heroin holders in the hills. Gun runners in rural areas. The streets live in many places.

Street life isn't always born from broken homes or poverty. Sometimes it's born from ambition, ego, greed, curiosity, secrecy, or the need to create a villain or a legend out of oneself. Some of the most ruthless people I've met weren't raised in scarcity—they were raised in excess. That excess didn't keep them out of the streets. It only amplified their reach within it.

Yes, street life, arguably, may have started in communities like the ones I grew up in. But it didn't die there. It evolved from the poorest Italian, Jewish, Latino, Asian, Samoan, white, and Black communities. It traded alleyways for gated driveways, swapped crack houses for condos, and found new homes in places no one suspects. I've met people from those places. Some were just as "dignified" as Obama.

Still, this myth gives society an excuse to look away. It lets suburban parents, school boards, and local officials believe, "That can't happen here. That won't happen here." But it can, it did, and it does. Because street culture is a mindset. A language. A survival code. A middle finger to "normal society." It's not just a location—it's a culture that has swept across the US for over a hundred years.

There's a privilege in believing that drugs, gangs, violence, and crime are merely infections from "lower-class" environments. It allows people to ignore the real issues: disconnection, mental health, identity, masculinity, trauma, and the need for purpose. Blaming poor neighborhoods keeps the truth buried.

Street life has never just been about where you live. It's about what lives in you, what you believe, how you see your future, how you see the system, whom you surround yourself with, and what you think you can get away with—human ambition—or what you are willing to trade, sacrifice, or destroy to feel like you matter.

THE TRUTH

Street life transcends social class and the environments it originates from. Once defined by gangs, guns, and crime, it has evolved into a culture that permeates every corner of society. It is no longer confined to race, education, or financial status, nor limited by upbringing or religious beliefs. Instead, street life has become a cultural force intertwined with mainstream society—a language of slang with countless dialects, adopted and celebrated even by those once considered "decent folk." While it remains a dangerous culture, its influence extends far beyond crime, shaping identities and narratives in ways that defy its origins.

STREET LIFE EXISTS ACROSS ALL SOCIAL CLASSES.

MYTH 4

THE "G CODE" GOVERNS THE STREETS

> The G Code is a universal, unshakable standard, a set of rules that must not be defied. It binds and governs the streets, ensures survival and honor, and creates respect among those in street life. Breaking the code is the ultimate betrayal, resulting in severe consequences ranging from loss of respect to violence or even death. The G Code is the backbone of the criminal world, which rules street culture. It's a badge of honor—a code of ethics that keeps everyone in check, separates "the real from the fake."

Before delving into this discussion, it is important to define the term *G Code* for those unfamiliar with its supposed meaning. The G Code, short for Gangster's Code, refers to a set of principles or rules that individuals immersed in street life are expected to follow. These principles often revolve around loyalty, respect, and honor, but their interpretation and application vary depending on the individual or group invoking them. No matter what, though, a principle of silence and loyalty always applies, and it is shameful to betray even your enemy—similar to the Mafia's code of *omertà*.

You can find this same concept echoed in the way nations interact on a global scale. A vast, complex body of rules, principles, orders, and diplomacy has been established between allies and adversaries alike to govern behavior in times of peace and conflict, forming the basis of international law. One of the most well-known examples of this is the Geneva Conventions—the international version of the G Code—which serves as the legal standard for the humane treatment of soldiers, prisoners, and civilians during wartime. The Geneva Conventions are designed to provide structure in chaos, setting boundaries even amid violence. Similarly, the streets operate under their own informal but deeply understood code of conduct meant to uphold order, respect, and survival. Like the Geneva Conventions or international law, the streets' G Code includes unwritten expectations or rules of engagement—such as family and children being off-limits—and violating them can lead to serious, even deadly, consequences. And just as international law punishes war crimes, or is supposed to, some street gangs and organizations will discipline or eliminate their own members if they break the code even accidentally, reinforcing a system where loyalty and order are protected at all costs.

In the same way, law enforcement across the nation's cities and states has its own version of a G Code—the infamous Blue Code of Silence. This widely known but unwritten rule discourages officers from exposing the misconduct or crimes of their colleagues, even when those acts directly violate the very laws they swore to uphold. Breaking this code can mean being ostracized, retaliated against, or worse. It is loyalty above law, silence above truth. This "code within a code" makes them no different than street soldiers who protect their own, even at the expense of justice, fueling rampant criminality within law enforcement and deepening the divide between communities and society at large. Just as the streets create boundaries to preserve power and survival, the police maintain their own shield of secrecy to protect their fraternity, their crafted image of "heroism," and all its ill-gotten gains, often blurring the line between order and corruption. As the Blue Code of Silence violates both federal and state laws and undermines public trust, it reveals a crucial difference from the G Code. While the G Code thrives in open, raw aggression, intimidation, and displays of dominance, the Blue Code conceals itself in bureaucracy, procedure, and the appearance of legitimacy. One survives in raw confrontation, the other in quiet cover-ups—yet both ultimately protect their own at the expense of truth and justice.

Codes like these aren't unique to the streets or the police—they have existed throughout history, in every corner of society where loyalty and survival outweighed written law. The G Code, for example, can be likened to what was once known as the Pirate Code, dating back centuries. Between the 1600s and 1800s, pirates—renowned for their acts of robbery, murder, plunder, and war—operated outside the bounds of society. They lived on their own terms, rejecting the norms of "civil society" and forming loose-knit communities with their own codes of conduct that reigned supreme. These codes, though often informal and unwritten, served as crucial guidelines for resolving disputes, maintaining order, and ensuring cooperation within their crews—a concept reflected throughout history and echoed in popular media such as *Pirates of the Caribbean*, *One Piece*, and *Black Sails*.

Similarly, modern street gangs, particularly those that

emerged early on in America's urban landscapes, had sought to establish their own codes to make themselves more than common hoodlums and thugs. A handful of organizations—such as the Gangster Disciples, founded by Larry Hoover; El Rukns/the Black P. Stones, founded by Jeff Fort; and the Black Disciples, founded by David Barksdale (better known as "King David")—went as far as drafting written rules to govern their members. These groups would form codes and laws under what are known as the five- and six-point stars. These documents aimed to instill discipline, promote unity, craft lessons, build a philosophy, and establish a sense of purpose beyond individual ambition—giving each member a sense of dignity to see themselves as more than a common gangbanger. They also outlined expectations for handling disputes, maintaining a chain of command, and upholding member integrity. Such guidelines fostered a sense of collective pride and identity within the group. Each member had to learn these rules and codes, store them mentally, and recite them on command if demanded by a higher authority within the organization. Some form of discipline would follow if they could not do so. They survived by their rules, and if the rules failed, then everything cracked and crumbled.

"For 25 years, I have had a front-row seat to the passing by of the World. I have consistently followed the news and current events, particularly those at home back in Chicago, and I can see the effect and consequences my past actions have contributed to. Even if at one time I had erroneously believed that my activities would somehow morph into a legit, benevolent organization, the underlying effects ultimately acted as a brake upon the actual progress that might have otherwise occurred."

—LARRY HOOVER, FOUNDER OF THE GANGSTER DISCIPLES, FROM HIS LETTER TO THE PUBLIC

However, as the prevalence of street gangs increased across the country, the formal structure of these codes began to erode. Written codes, wherever they may have existed, often collapsed under the weight of internal conflicts, weak members, and/or the aggressive intervention of law enforcement. Federal indictments targeting leaders dismantled hierarchical structures, leaving many groups without leadership and a cohesive framework to enforce their rules. This created a power vacuum and led to erratic behavior among their members. This is a military tactic of killing the head and watching the body fall. It was observed that the rise in crime and deaths occurred in environments that hadn't experienced such effects when internal order and discipline were enforced among its members. But as J. Edgar Hoover (the first director of the FBI) once noted, "Justice is merely incidental to law and order."

Over time, the G Code became a set of expectations passed down verbally from person to person, often without consistency or clarity. This word-of-mouth transmission opened the door for individual interpretations, with each person redefining what the G Code meant to them. What was once a self-regulating structure—tight-knit and almost sacred—began to erode. The exclusivity that once defined the streets gave way to chaos; anyone could claim to live by the code without truly understanding its roots. As street life became glamorized, commodified, and monetized through music, movies, and media, the G Code lost its mystique. It had been a code of silence and loyalty known only to insiders, but it became public knowledge, paraded on the evening news, and blared through the speakers of mainstream culture. The code wasn't just broken—it was broadcast. As Peter Zuccaro, a Gambino associate who turned informant against John Gotti, once put it, "He publicized everything that was going on. He brought everything that was supposed to be a secret society right out to the forefront, right into the press."

The term *G Code* might be as old as organized crime itself. It has morphed across eras, cultures, and communities, meant to create order among all those who operate outside the law, whether gangster or not.

For example, as the prison population grew and gangsters became the most prominent figures in prison, the G Code became consolidated. Living by the code became the norm, and prisoners who were not affiliated with gang life became subject to the G Code when it came to things like snitching, child molestation, or rape. Those acts and crimes were treated as unforgivable and often met with harsh punishments or even death. The code dictated which acts or crimes, even committed by an "average Joe," were tolerable and which were abhorrent.

Over time, as the streets became more divided—by race, drugs, poverty, power, and oppression—the code splintered too. Everybody interpreted it in their own way. Its values got diluted. Its enforcement became inconsistent. Leaders were self-appointed. Order became chaos. Street life became a free-for-all. "Crazy" became cool. Recklessness was respected. And bullets replaced boundaries. This wasn't confined to just one corner of street life—it was happening across many parts of it. As Tommaso Buscetta, a former Mafia member, once said, "I have seen our organization change from within. I have seen money, drugs, and greed corrupt the Cosa Nostra code of honor and loyalty to the families. I decided to cooperate with the Italian and American authorities in part because I felt the Mafia I had known no longer existed."

The G Code became just a name. A phrase. A ghost.

It haunts the culture, but it doesn't necessarily govern it because most street affiliates aren't really willing to die for it.

Those who often find themselves betrayed by the very people who say they stand for it too.

The G Code, like the Pirate Code before it, was designed to establish order within chaos. However, in the face of internal and external pressures in every facet of street life, its authority has largely dissolved. Today, in most urban street gangs, the code of conduct exists more as a nostalgic symbol than a genuine set of principles. The myth of the G Code persists as each person or crew interprets it through their own lens, twisting it to fit their circumstances. But its original meaning—the totality of what it once stood for—has faded, leaving behind scattered fragments and contradicting ideals that no longer form a solid foundation in the evolving landscape of street life.

Yet the influence of the G Code still lingers. It continues to shape the mindset of those immersed in street culture and newcomers, becoming the hidden framework behind many of the twenty-one myths explored throughout this book. Loyalty, masculinity, antigayness, power, trust, dedication, and respect are not isolated concepts—they're fragments of this larger belief system regarding the code. So, when the G Code fractures, it sets off a domino effect—its power to govern is a fragile myth, taking one rule down at a time. Many will deny this because they need something to continue to hold on to, but others will agree because they recognized this long ago and let go of the code.

The G Code, once considered sacred, became diluted, leaving code and its power to govern a myth—a remnant of an idealized past rather than a functioning reality.

STREET VIEW

When I was growing up, there was an old saying our parents used to repeat to us: "Birds of a feather flock together." It usually pointed to the friends we kept and the choices we made with them. It reflected who we were or who we were trying to be. Surprisingly—or maybe not—this same idea applied to those in street life. But in a world built on rebellion and chaos, what is it that actually keeps people flocking together? What forges those tight bonds between people who live outside the law? What governs loyalty, defines betrayal, and sets the standards for what's right or wrong?

In the streets, the answer to those questions is simple:
The G Code.
But what is the G Code?
As far back as I can remember, I wanted to know. Truthfully, as a kid, I became more eager to understand the G Code than I ever was to learn the words—or the meaning—of the Pledge of Allegiance. School felt optional. But the G Code? That felt essential. I began to see street life as a potential destiny. And with every passing day, the possibility became more plausible. So I wanted to know everything, from the ground up.

I started asking questions. I went to OGs and BGs from every neighborhood I lived in. I asked, "What is the G Code?"

Some would light up, proud to pass something down like a father to a son. Others grew uncomfortable, unsure how to answer. But even with all the frustration and contradictions, two answers rose to the top:

No snitching.
Respect.

Respect was treated like royalty. It was the street's version of heaven—something every man hoped for after surviving hell. It often came with or gave access to money, power, and women—

the holy trinity of street success, and maybe of life in general. But oddly enough, disrespect seemed to get more applause. Respect wasn't handed out easily, no matter how respectfully you acted. Self-interest, murder, robbery, betrayal, and intimidation had a tendency to outshine honor. Aggression became the true language of survival. Either you were aggressive or you defended yourself aggressively. Jungle law seemed to rule. Eye contact could easily spark a fight. Accidentally brushing up on someone could quickly end in a shooting. Even a well-timed apology usually arrived too late. Fighters were honored. Shooters were glorified. Diplomacy could easily be misinterpreted as backing down. Violence was currency. Respect was unstable. And if there was one thing that was supposed to be nonnegotiable, it was respect.

Then there's no snitching—the supposed golden rule. The mother of all codes. The most recognizable standard of the streets. This was repeated so loudly and so often that even outsiders believed in it. But over time, the shine wore off. The rule that was once absolute started to rust. People began justifying it, explaining it away. Some even started scheduling when they thought it was okay to snitch.

Phrases like "He didn't rat on me, so I ain't trippin" became popular. Snitching wasn't seen as a universal betrayal anymore—it was judged case by case, like a court ruling. And when people began bending the code, no one stepped up to enforce it. Snitches were rarely if ever exiled, beaten, or killed, at least on the streets—they were ignored, tolerated, even befriended. The house was a mess, and no one wanted to take out the trash or keep the door shut to stop the flies from coming in. The commandments had been broken, and everyone still wanted to sip from the Holy Grail.

I've heard people justify snitching in all kinds of ways: "I'd do it if my moms was in danger" or "if my kid's life depended on it." I've even heard some people justifying the rapper 6ix9ine's act of snitching.

Every person who said those things was exiled from my life. Not because I was trying to be some upholder of the code, but because I couldn't respect the contradiction. These same people would brag about loyalty one minute, then defend betrayal the next. The truth nobody wants to say out loud is this:

The G Code, for many, only works when it's convenient.

For some, the G no longer stands for gangster—it stands for grimy, greedy, gutless.

Because when things get real, it's not the code that kicks in. It's fear. Pressure. Ego. Survival. Self-interest. Many who claim to live by principles will betray those principles the moment they're forced to choose between the code and themselves.

I started to see, maybe a little too late, why street life stays chaotic. People constantly teeter between being "real," being entertained, or just "being in the moment." Street life became a stage, maybe long before I was born, and the G Code became part of the set design. A backdrop. A costume. People would step in, sit down, pose, and then go home or head to their nine-to-five when the lights turned off.

The G Code once symbolized something sacred: death before dishonor or falling on your sword. Now it's become a slogan without a spine. People violate the code quietly and justify it loudly. Eventually, the whole thing starts to unravel. The code becomes a con, a myth, a fairy tale to give newcomers hope of something better than where they come from. Then it becomes the weapon people only use when it works in their favor.

And just like that, the street brotherhood starts to look less like unity and more like *Lord of the Flies*.

Where once even enemies held to the same code—"respectable enemies," they were proud to be called—now it's all out in the open. What happens in the streets doesn't stay in the streets anymore. It's a soap opera, with livestreams and confessions to outsiders. People crave the approval of those who used to be called wannabes. The code has been handed over to the pop culture department. The G Code became a fad.

Many have walked away, not because they're cowards, but because they finally admitted the truth:

The G Code doesn't govern anything anymore—not for the vast majority of the streets.

It was supposed to bring honor where there was none, offer dignity where it seemed impossible, and control chaos with a code. But honor, when it's inconvenient, becomes hard to hold. Heavy to carry.

And the harsh truth? Codes, laws, and rules are only as strong as the people willing to live by them.

People break rules everywhere—religious rules, family rules, corporate rules. Even the world's most powerful nations bend or ignore their own standards. Take international law, for example: protocols like the Geneva Conventions are meant to preserve a shred of humanity in times of war. Yet those very nations that helped draft them are often the first to violate them. The same contradiction shows up in policing. Officers raise their right hand and swear to uphold the written laws, but with the other hand—fingers crossed behind their back—they quietly pledge allegiance to a different code, one of silence and loyalty above truth.

I started to notice it wasn't much different in a life of crime. The G Code was the street's Geneva Convention or code of silence. It was meant to maintain some form of respect, even in violence, and set boundaries, even in war. But just like international law, it's only as strong as those who enforce it. Break the rules, and the whole system bends. The whole thing becomes performative—an illusion dressed in loyalty.

Still, we all develop our own codes, our own personal politics. Often, they clash with the groups we're a part of or the world we live in, but we keep them. We live by them when we can.

Every now and then, life deals us a bad hand—and when it does, our codes stare us in the face.

But all of us have a few aces up our sleeves.

Whether we stick to our code or play an ace—that choice is ours alone.

> **THE TRUTH**
>
> Rules, regulations, and codes of conduct are created by those seeking to impose order and control. Yet the human desire for self-governance often leads people to deviate from these rules to live as they see fit. When the structures or institutions that uphold a code are weak or broken, the code itself becomes harder to enforce, sustain, or even believe in. Ultimately, a code of conduct is only as strong as the individuals or groups committed to upholding it. As self-reliance becomes normalized or celebrated, the stability of rules unravels, leaving people to rely on fragile hope that others will still follow them. This is what you might call a hope code. You're hoping others won't snitch you out or break any other rules.

TO BE GOVERNED BY MYTHS IS TO LIVE IN FICTION.

MYTH 5

CARRYING A GUN IS ESSENTIAL TO STREET LIFE

> Carrying a gun in street life is not a choice; it's a must. It is better to be caught with a gun by the police than to be caught without a gun by a rival. There are no other choices in this life we live. You make a move before your enemies do. It's the only way to keep yourself, your family, and the hood safe. Anyone who disagrees will die early.

When we think of street life, danger is often one of the first things that comes to mind. It is a world where survival often hinges on a delicate balance of self-reliance and hyperawareness. It is a life of crime in an environment where trust is scarce, death seems inevitable, and barbaric behavior is normalized—making the concept of danger not only obvious but central to existence. Against this backdrop, carrying a gun might appear to be essential—a rational response to the ever-present threat of harm. However, the reality is far more complex and tragic.

The presence of a firearm often escalates conflicts that might otherwise be resolved through dialogue, avoidance, or even a fistfight. A gun changes the dynamics of a dispute, encouraging hyperaggression and amplifying egos. For many, the weapon ceases to be a tool for protection and instead becomes a symbol of power and intimidation, often altering character and judgment. Instead of de-escalating danger, a gun often invites it, turning tense moments into fatal ones. As rapper Tech N9ne once reflected, firearms and the criminal underworld are persistent realities, but it's often poor judgment and recklessness that turn them deadly. His point is clear: guns by themselves don't define the culture; how they're used does.

But the impact of this myth—the belief that carrying a gun is essential to street life—extends far beyond the streets. It infiltrates society at large, shaping mindsets and behaviors in ways that perpetuate cycles of violence. A child raised in an environment where guns are glorified as necessary for survival is more likely to internalize this belief. They'll grow up equating power and safety with the possession of a firearm, often perpetuating the same dangers that once threatened them. This undermines their ability to form trust, build honest connections, and develop healthy social behaviors, leading to a breakdown in individual well-being and communal stability. Over time, this power dynamic creates a distorted understanding of control and respect until roles reverse and the once-vulnerable individual becomes the aggressor.

This myth, more than many others, is uniquely insidious. It spawns sub-myths that further entrench its narrative in the culture of street life. These sub-myths—smaller beliefs that fall under the broader myth—are varied but share a common thread of distortion:

- **"Anyone who carries a gun will use it to kill"**: In reality, most individuals in street life do not discharge their weapons, even when their lives are in danger. The myth exaggerates the intent behind carrying a gun, ignoring the complexities of fear, hesitation, and human restraint.
- **"Guns make you a gangster"**: This belief perpetuates the dangerous idea that a firearm is a badge of authenticity or status in the streets. It encourages performative violence, often for the validation of peers or onlookers. Tragically, children and impressionable individuals absorb these displays, believing that carrying a gun is a mark of character or strength, only to later realize they were shaped by falsehoods and hollow bravado.
- **"A gun is a problem solver"**: This sub-myth is particularly dangerous because it suggests that violence is the quickest and most effective way to resolve conflict. It fosters impulsive behavior, encouraging people to be reactive rather than proactive, with little thought to the long-term consequences of their actions.
- **"It's better to be caught with it than caught without it"**: The "it," of course, is the gun, and this is perhaps the most famous of these beliefs. This sub-myth prioritizes immediate action over long-term consequences. The logic seems sound on the surface—better to face jail time than to possibly be harmed as a result of being unable to defend oneself—but it disregards the harsh realities of legal repercussions. Laws like the Armed Career Criminal Act (ACCA) and similar state statutes can lead to decades of incarceration for possession of a firearm, a reality that many in street life are unaware of until it's too late.

In street life, guns are often idolized like modern-day golden calves. The gun becomes an object of reverence, and the myths surrounding it serve as sacred scriptures, guiding behavior and justifying violence. Urban legends, movies, music, and the rhetoric of false prophets amplify these narratives, framing the gun as a divine force—a rod and staff that provides power, salvation, and retribution.

This mythological reverence creates a cycle of premature and irresponsible gun ownership. Individuals eager to assert dominance or protect their reputations wield firearms, with little understanding of the consequences. The result is an unrelenting rise in violence, with lives lost every day. Victims become martyrs or legends, their names etched on tombstones, their faces printed on T-shirts, their monikers tattooed on bodies, and their stories retold in ways that glorify their deaths rather than mourn their unnecessary loss. Yet as time passes, memories of them fade, replaced by new tragedies, unresolved conflicts, and lingering regrets.

The glorification of guns in street life is deeply intertwined with America's broader culture of violence. Since the nation's inception, firearms have been central to its identity, used to conquer, control, and assert dominance both at home and abroad. The Second Amendment, guaranteeing "the right to bear arms," has only fueled this fascination, embedding the gun in America's collective psyche. Over generations, this obsession has trickled down into subcultures like street life, where the gun continues to be both a symbol of survival and a tool of destruction. It is even seen as a part of the family, a guide or a guardian that is iterated, glorified, and glamourized in many songs, especially in rap music, such as "My Buddy" by G-Unit. The song depicts the gun as a need, and not necessarily a lawful one, as street life doesn't care about gun laws, only the so-called pride and use of them.

In the end, the myth that carrying a gun is essential to street life is not just about survival; it is about power, perception, and identity. It is a myth that feeds on fear and thrives on ignorance, perpetuating a cycle of violence that leaves no winners, only a slew of casualties. To challenge this myth is to challenge the very foundations of street life and the narratives that sustain it. And because street life is driven by many things—including fear, bullying, emotions, and myths—this will be a myth that's hard to battle.

STREET VIEW

When I was twenty-five years old—the same age Tupac was when he was shot to death—the sounds of police sirens, helicopters, and gunfire had become a soundtrack to many lives, including my own. Back then, the sounds of bullets rang out like fireworks on the Fourth of July. Tragedy was normalized. "Who's next?" was the quiet question we carried. In some regards, not much has changed. Guns are still assumed to be the only answer—a must-have, like water to life: a need, not a want.

In street life, guns aren't just tools—they're trophies, totems, and sometimes even therapists. For many of us growing up in crime, carrying a gun became part of the uniform of the streets—not just to survive the war, but to prove we were part of it. Even for those who faked it, it still added to their image. The gun offered an identity, insinuated manhood, raised our voices, and demanded respect. Usually the gun was bigger than the person who was toting it or the hands that tried to grip it.

For a short man like myself, who grew up feeling bullied and underestimated, a gun leveled the playing field. It gave me stature in a world where size, strength, and savagery often dictated respect. If you had encountered me in the streets, with my hand on my gun, daring anyone to match my negative energy, "What chu say, nigga!?" could have been the last words you heard.

In environments where fists can only swing so far and rational words get drowned out by anger and pride, the gun spoke the loudest—and bullets reached the furthest. Unfortunately, sometimes the gun spoke first, and your point could be heard from blocks away.

I hated arguing, I hated drama, and above all I hated violence, but the gun became my insurance policy against all of it—the bullying, the threats. It was a tool of last resort that quietly, dangerously, sadly would become my first response if I had it on me.

I was the "getting money" type, and when the money starts flowing and your name begins to carry weight, the fear of losing it all starts to outweigh the joy of even having it. So the gun becomes not just protection—it becomes the answer to every threat, real or imagined. But here's the twist nobody talks about: the more often you carry a gun, the more likely you are to need it, to use it—not because danger increases, but because your own paranoia does. Your own assumption that "you must" wield it becomes a cultural addiction, especially when you're dealing with unspoken and unresolved issues, not only from others but from within yourself. You become the danger. The weapon you carry becomes the weapon you might one day use unconsciously to destroy everything you care about, including yourself. You and the gun become symbiotic; I know this through experience.

But here's where it gets deeper:

Sometimes the gun is demanded—due to fear, survival, or the real dangers lurking on the streets. But other times, the gun is commanded—due to culture, ego, or the unspoken rules of manhood and image. It's not just about being safe—it's about being seen, feared, and respected. Whether you need the gun or not doesn't always matter. The myth says you do, so you listen, and it becomes the go-to in most situations.

I didn't just notice this in myself. I saw it in others. Pride plus a gun can contradict the wise. Trauma plus a weapon can justify irrational responses. Loyalty becomes questionable. Conversations get louder. Points of view undoubtedly become one-sided. And reasonably or not, the gun becomes the final decision—even when the heart hasn't had time to think things through. This effect is compounded by onlookers and instigators or concern about what others may think of you.

This becomes the crossroads between war and wisdom, essentiality and choice. Even when we know better, there's no guarantee we'll do better. Knowledge is like a gun; it's only powerful when you show it or use it.

Street life destabilizes everything around us. When we consume too much of it, our minds become like a seesaw—rising with joy one moment, then crashing down in rage the next. Balance is difficult to maintain.

Undoubtedly, I have seen it. Some choose firepower over friendship, silence over communication, and arrogance over peace. But we could stop, think, recalibrate, check our egos. That alone could de-escalate situations. But the myth doesn't want us to pause. The myth accentuates the gun, elevates ignorance, and multiplies chaos. It's an adrenaline rush, an addiction, an assumed justification for those who sniff slogans like "stay strapped," "keep that thang on you," or "rather be caught with it than caught without it."

If carrying a gun were truly essential, then all those who carry them would never be harmed. But some are.

This proves that a gun can't promise survival—even when it's used.

Carrying a gun might be common in street life. But it's far from essential.

Communities have lost so many souls to this myth. Lives, futures, and mentalities are changed indefinitely, and the consequences and circumstances must be lived with forever.

Guns can—and usually do—escalate major, minor, and even nonthreatening situations, whether these involve strangers or law enforcement.

In federal detention centers, I've watched people return from court hearings with sentences ranging from five to fifteen years for nothing more than the simple possession of a handgun. I've met others later on in prison yards. And honestly, some of these individuals probably would've never even fired their weapon, even if their lives depended on it.

Carrying a gun might seem essential in street life—and for many, maybe it is. But an unhealthy mind and an unstable character plus a gun is a recipe for disaster. I started reminding myself that I had an unhealthy mind and an unstable character, and if I needed a gun just to exist somewhere, then maybe, just maybe, I didn't need to be there at all.

THE TRUTH

Guns tend to blur the line between protection and power, vulnerability and strength, restraint and reaction. The sense of invincibility that a gun provides is often a dangerous illusion of control. Many guns are never fired, but when they are, the act is often unnecessary and reckless, leading to consequences far beyond the intended purpose. By the time the shooter realizes that firing the gun wasn't essential in that moment, they are facing consequences or circumstances that cannot be undone, or, in most cases, forgiven.

CARRYING A GUN TENDS TO ESCALATE MATTERS.

―――― **MYTH 6** ――――

PEOPLE ONLY SNITCH OUT OF FEAR

> Fear of jail or prison is the driving force behind snitching—this is the very thing that defines a snitch. Cowardice takes priority over loyalty, motivating their betrayal. *They bitch-made, weak, and wasn't built for real shit anyways. Fear makes a snitch, and that's that!*

The most convenient explanation for why people only snitch is fear. However, this oversimplification fails to capture the complexity of motivations behind such an action. Many might dismiss this discussion altogether, arguing, "Who cares why someone snitched? They snitched!" Others might say, "The damage is already done—this isn't worth discussing." On the contrary, understanding why people snitch is crucial for deepening knowledge and educating both current and future generations about the unseen dangers of street life. By unpacking the diverse reasons for snitching, we can challenge harmful misconceptions, provide valuable insights, and offer tools to help people, especially young people, make better choices and avoid situations that may misguide them.

To address this myth, we must ask: why do people snitch if fear isn't the primary motivator? The answer lies in the complexity of survival. While fear is an emotional response to a perceived threat, survival is a primal instinct—the drive to overcome obstacles and secure physical, mental, emotional, or social well-being. Snitching, in this sense, becomes a tool for survival, wielded to reduce harm, regain control, or tilt circumstances in one's favor. At the core, long before morality kicks in, human behavior is often shaped by animal-like instincts—domination, self-preservation, and the urge to outlive threats. These instincts operate beneath emotions, including fear, influencing how people respond under pressure.

If fear alone were the driving force, then everyone—hardened criminals included—would snitch when faced with danger. Yet countless individuals in street life resist the temptation to betray, even when afraid. This resilience highlights that survival strategies vary widely and that fear, while significant, is often secondary to calculated self-preservation.

Snitching is not always about fear; at times, it's about position—strategizing for revenge, gaining favor with law enforcement, outwitting opponents, or eliminating competition. Take, for instance, what's known as "dry snitching"—the art of telling without telling. In street life, this usually comes as a "slick remark" dropped in conversation, made to sound casual or even loyal to the game, but crafted to put another person in the crosshairs. It can harm someone physically—by pushing them toward the heat of law enforcement—or socially, by planting doubt and suspicion among other peers. Unlike the snitch who cracks under pressure, the dry snitch operates willfully and deliberately, exposing others not out of fear but out of calculation. In a life of crime, these acts occur much more often than many realize, without coercion or fear as a motivating factor.

On the streets, loyalty, integrity, and honor are often upheld as core values, but for many, those values bend the moment their lifestyles, names, or very lives are at stake. Jay-Z's "A Week Ago," featuring Too $hort, captures this tension with his closest friend, who turned informant because he began to miss the lifestyle he once had. Similarly, Obie Trice's "Snitch," featuring Akon, underscores how quickly the code of silence can collapse even when you have known someone since childhood. In both cases, the idea of "doing what you have to do" overrides any internal sense of "street morality," exposing the disconnect between what someone claims to stand for and the actions they take in moments of crisis or opportunity.

Such contradictions are especially evident when individuals justify their betrayals as righteous. This highlights that, for some, morality is fluid—easily adapted to suit their immediate needs rather than being rooted in steadfast principles. These methodical acts, rooted in ambition rather than desperation, make such individuals some of the most dangerous players in the criminal world. Their betrayals are calculated and intentional, often leaving no trace and allowing them to operate undetected while furthering their own agendas.

The concept of snitching is nothing new. For centuries, stories have been told about betrayal and broken trust. One of the most well-known is the story of Jesus and Judas. Whether viewed as fact or fiction, it stands as a case in point: Judas cooperated not under threat of jail or fear of death, but out of greed for money, betraying Jesus with nothing more than a kiss (Matthew 26:48-50).

Fast-forward to modern times: snitching—arguably more effective than the wiretap—became one of law enforcement's greatest tools. In the 1980s, laws were enacted to encourage cooperation, offering reduced sentences and even payments for those who provided what was called "substantial assistance."

This shift directly challenged the old idea, attributed to the Roman writer Cicero, that "there is honor among thieves." Once the courts created rewards for betrayal, the code of silence was no longer just tested—it was systematically dismantled. Snitching stopped being merely an act of fear and began functioning like a job, a transaction. Mandatory minimums for drug offenses piled on immense pressure, leaving defendants with little choice but to cooperate if they wanted to avoid decades behind bars. Plea bargains, which traded information for lighter charges or reduced time, became the new norm, turning cooperation into a survival strategy across all levels of crime.

Over time, this reality gave rise to the darker, more cynical version of the proverb: "There is no honor among thieves." The reliance on snitches and informants transformed the modern drug war and all criminal activities into something resembling the Salem witch trials, where accusation became currency and survival meant pointing the finger before someone pointed it at you.

These actions and policies blurred the lines between fear and complex motivations, turning cooperation into a calculated tradeoff rather than an act of sheer panic or a moral choice. High- and low-level criminals alike began to see snitching as a viable tool for navigating the legal system and securing personal advantages.

Ultimately, the myth that snitches are driven solely by fear oversimplifies the complex motivations behind betrayal in street life. Fear is easier to accept as an explanation, as it reduces the act to a moment of weakness. However, snitching often involves calculated decisions in pursuit of power, money, position, or survival. By attributing snitching solely to fear, we risk ignoring the deeper truths about crime, survival, and the harsh realities of the streets and what it takes to navigate them.

Snitching is not just a simple act—it's a strategy, a tool wielded with precision, and a reflection of the broader dynamics of power and self-preservation. Recognizing this complexity is essential for understanding the intricate web of motivations that drive individuals in the shadowy corners of society.

This discussion isn't about promoting, vilifying, or diminishing snitching—it's about acknowledging the myth and exposing the many reasons for betrayal, opportunistic behavior, and the motivations behind it. It's about providing insight to the youth and others who choose to enter or operate in street life blindly, assuming that their "friends," "homies," or "family" will never use this tool against them.

STREET VIEW

"I seen it all. So ain't shit about street life you can tell me," I used to say with pride. And for a long time, I truly believed it. I believed I had seen every twist and turn the streets had to offer—until I realized there was one corner of street life I'd stayed willfully ignorant of:

The snitches. And the many reasons behind their actions.

I never really got to know this part of the game in depth, mainly because I made it a point to stay away from snitches. I kept my distance at all costs, proving that you can't learn much if you don't know much. Trying to be "real," I did myself a great deal of disservice. Even so, I had strong opinions. I used to believe that anyone who snitched did it because they were afraid of prison and all that came with it—the fights, the stabbings, the constant defense, even the possibility of being raped. Or just simply losing the lifestyle they had grown accustomed to—the money, the assumed freedom, their children and the women in their lives.

And for some, maybe that was the truth. Maybe fear was the reason. But over time, I learned that for others, snitching was something far more calculated—strategic even. There was a kind of mastery to it. An art. And that realization shattered a belief I had carried for over thirty years in street life.

When I was coming up, the life I started to idolize and the gangsters I looked up to never pulled me aside to explain this part of the streets. Snitches were simply ridiculed and written off—called weak, soft, "bitch-made ass niggas." They were the bottom of the barrel in a life that was already beneath society's barrel. In the street code, it was stamped as fact: men only snitched because they were scared and didn't want to deal with "real gangsta shit."

And maybe once upon a time that was totally true. Who knows. But like all things in the game, snitching evolved. Old rules became outdated, and the players rewrote the script.

My own bravado—how "real," how "solid," how "gangsta" I thought I was—blinded me from seeing this evolution. That same pride had me feeling untouchable, convinced that the streets only belonged to the "real ones." That mindset didn't just make me ignorant; it left me vulnerable. I got ratted out multiple times. Two of these landed me in prison—once in state, then in federal.

No matter how nervous, worried, or flat-out terrified I was,

I kept my mouth shut. "Never let 'em see you sweat," they say—but believe me, I was sweating, like a motherfucker! Every arrest. Every courtroom. Every time I stood in front of a judge, knowing I was about to lose everything that mattered to me—my kids, their mothers, the money, the life, my "freedom"—I felt it all. The fear was real.

Still, I never ratted. I'd be lying if I said I never considered it. Once—just once—the thought crossed my mind. The feds laid their offers on the table, and for a split second, I actually thought about what it would be like to take it. I mean, it came with many more perks than simply keeping me out of jail, and I took the offer as a compliment. But it didn't sit right in my spirit. I knew what I had signed up for when I stepped into "the life." The pain, the prison time, the distance from my children, before they were even born—that was all part of the contract—at least the one I signed. Fear was part of the game. I had to learn to live with it, just as those before me—the ones that I respected and idolized—had.

What I learned in state and federal lockup confirmed something deeper: not everyone snitches out of fear. Some do it for freedom, yes. But others do it for control.

Take gang dropouts, for example. I learned that these are people who could have been in gang life all their lives and instead decided to walk away—not necessarily because they're scared, but because they want to change. They might cooperate with authorities because they're seeking a different life. I saw that with my own eyes—dudes who debriefed, who told it all willingly. Not to avoid a beatdown. Not because of threats. But because they wanted out. They chose to live under threat and be who they wanted to be rather than live under the protection of who they no longer were.

Snitching didn't necessarily make people soft. Some of those same guys would still throw hands, still stand their ground. In the federal detention center, I knew of a snitch who beat up his co-defendants, the very people that he snitched out. His co-defendants assumed he was snitching out of fear, confronted him with the intent to harm him, and unfortunately found out the hard way.

That's when I started to understand that snitching doesn't make you less of a man—it just removes you from a certain group, shamefully or proudly. If you don't understand that difference, you might pay the price for it.

For example, look at what reportedly happened with Nipsey Hussle. Word is, he called Eric Holder a snitch. That confrontation ended with Nipsey's death. Whether or not Holder actually was a snitch is left for the streets to debate. For those who adamantly say Holder was a snitch, at least this shows that snitching doesn't always equal fear—and it damn sure shows that a snitch would pull a trigger.

Snitching, in some cases, is a performance. A power move. A role played with intention. I learned that it can be revenge disguised as loyalty, betrayal disguised as necessity. It's survival of the fittest in its most twisted form.

Take James "Whitey" Bulger—an American mob boss who worked as a "Top Echelon Informant" for a couple of corrupt FBI agents. He wasn't pressured into it. He wasn't scared. He made a conscious choice to snitch on rivals in exchange for protection, information, and power. He used snitching as a weapon to wipe out competition, and in return, he was allowed to run his criminal empire unchecked. That's not fear. That's strategy.

There are plenty more like him on the streets, in the hood, and behind closed doors. I've met some of them—people who openly work with top-level law enforcement and still commit crimes like it's nothing. They use snitching as a power play, out of greed, jealousy, or ambition. When I asked one of them why he did it, he said, "Street life has no honor." And with a straight face, he said, "Look at me." I tried to convince him that he could get caught and go to prison, and snitching couldn't save him. His reply was simply, "I'll worry about prison if or when it comes."

It reminded me of one of the most comical but true lines in street culture:

"I'ma drop a dime on them niggas."

It sounds like a joke, but it happens every day. Quietly and anonymously, without pressure, people inform on their rivals, using the law as their personal enforcer to avoid direct dealings with brute or friendly competition.

It hit me that this was a different type of scandalous, a different type of snake, but still a player in the game. Snitches come in all forms—loud and quiet, male and female, and all races. They have different names: rats, CIs, canaries, squealers, stool pigeons. But no matter the title, they all play an intricate role in the streets.

The funny thing is that the streets love to act like there is "honorable dirt," while a snitch's dirt is dishonorable. But dirt is dirt. Betrayal is betrayal. Disrespect is disrespect. And a snake is a snake. So as I walked the path of a so-called stand-up man—through the streets, jails, federal and state prisons, and back again—I started seeing things more clearly.

Not in a way that made me wish I had snitched, but in a way that made me understand this:

Snitching is just another monster, a nightmare among others. And it isn't always about fear. Often it's about opportunity. Sometimes it's strategic—a calculated move. People cooperate with law enforcement not just to save themselves but to gain leverage, eliminate competition, or maintain power while appearing powerless.

In that light, the snitch isn't just a traitor—they're a survivor, a manipulator, a player of systems. And in some cases, they're more in control than the people they betray. These individuals aren't trembling in back rooms—they're fearless, self-serving, and Machiavellian. They'll double-cross the streets and the government alike—and anyone else. They are loyal to nothing but their own ambition. For them, snitching becomes a weapon, like a gun used against an enemy. They use their cooperation to sabotage rivals, build false narratives, and stay relevant in the underworld without feeling like they are getting their hands dirty—it kind of reminds me of *The Penguin* on HBO.

This shows that snitches are not always cowards. Some aren't flipping because they're afraid. They're flipping because it keeps them in the game. It gives them value and keeps them alive in a world in which they know they can't or won't ever obtain a certain level of power—but they still want to be part of.

Snitching has evolved far beyond the image of a scared man in an interrogation room, sweating bullets and begging for mercy. Some informants today are career players—CIs with long-term agreements, multiple income streams, and ties to both sides of the law. They are rich. They are poor. They are everywhere.

So yes, some snitches snitch because they're scared—but don't get it twisted. Many snitch because it works. Because it pays. Because it gives them a power they could never gain on the streets alone. And sometimes they do it simply because they can; they know the people that they're snitching on won't do anything about it. In fact, some even end up back around the same people they snitched out—hanging around, doing business, laughing like nothing ever happened. It sounds wild, but it's real. I've seen it.

This isn't about showing respect to snitches. And it's not

about blindly hating them either. The myth protects street affiliates from the harder truth: betrayal isn't always born from weakness, regret, or a desire to do right. Sometimes it's rooted in cold strategy—and that's more dangerous than fear will ever be.

> **THE TRUTH**
>
> When we overlook a person's will to survive, we dismiss a fundamental aspect of human nature—the innate desire to live comfortably and securely. Our hopes for love, loyalty, and partnership often overshadow the harsh truth that life operates according to survival of the fittest. Survival isn't always driven by visible fear; it is equally fueled by ambition, greed, and manipulation. These motivations may be less acknowledged, but they are just as integral to human behavior, shaping decisions in ways we rarely admit.

THE MOTIVATIONS BEHIND SNITCHING ARE COMPLEX.

─── **MYTH 7** ───

STREET MONEY IS EASY MONEY

> Street money offers a shortcut to societal norms, an easy path to top financial success without the constraints of traditional work or education. Street money requires little to no effort, skills, or time compared to conventional jobs that are demanding or useless in acquiring the means to build an empire. There are no taxes, so all the money you make is yours. It's easy, so why not do it?

Street money, and the myth that it is easy to obtain, has been a Venus flytrap for Americans for over one hundred years. The allure of quick riches has ensnared generations, but the roots of this myth are deeply embedded in history. The rise of street culture and its underground wealth dates back to the late nineteenth century and early twentieth century, during the Industrial Revolution, when urban neighborhoods began to take shape—the beginnings of what would come to be known as street life.

The Prohibition era of the 1920s further fueled the notion that "crime pays," as organized crime flourished and the first illegal liquor operations were developed, from manufacturing and distribution to nightclubs, or speakeasies. Even John D. Rockefeller—oil tycoon and, at that time, the wealthiest man in the world—was forced to acknowledge the unintended consequences of trying to legislate morality. Reflecting on the fallout of Prohibition, he wrote, "When Prohibition was introduced, I hoped that it would be widely supported by public opinion and the day would soon come when the evil effects of alcohol would be recognized. I have slowly and reluctantly come to believe that this has not been the result. Instead, drinking has generally increased; the speakeasy has replaced the saloon; a vast army of lawbreakers has appeared; many of our best citizens have openly ignored Prohibition; respect for the law has greatly lessened; and crime has increased to a level never seen before."

Illicit establishments became a cornerstone of street culture, defying segregation and welcoming men and women of all races, including members of the LGBTQ+ community (before it was known as such). As Charles "Lucky" Luciano (an Italian American gangster and the founder of the Commission) once said, "There's no such thing as good money or bad money. There's just money." In many of these spaces, money was equal before it was equal in the eyes of the law. Crime, for a time, appeared to be a great equalizer. This era solidified the belief that crime did pay, as these once-illicit and "ungodly" activities were eventually legitimized. Some would even argue that the government and corporations stole ideas and practices from the American mob and later weaved them into American culture.

The underworld economy in America was largely dominated by immigrant communities—primarily Italian, Irish, Jewish, and Eastern European. In the late nineteenth and early twentieth centuries, poverty, discrimination, and limited access to opportunity pushed many of these marginalized groups into illicit trades as a means of survival and social mobility. Street money was far from easy then—it was bloodstained and earned through dangerous ventures like illegal gambling, brothels, racketeering, and most infamously, bootlegging during Prohibition. These were industries governed by fear, corruption, and homicide, where influence often mattered as much as firepower. As Al Capone famously said, "You can go a long way with a smile—but a lot farther with a smile and a gun."

Organized crime families ruled neighborhoods with iron fists, and police corruption and its brutality ran rampant—as it does today—offering protection for the "right price." Street money was not easy, and murder rates soared as organized crime began to take root in American cities, giving rise to powerful, brutal syndicates. The Italian Mafia, Irish mobs, Jewish gangs, and other ethnic criminal networks fought bloody territorial wars, turning neighborhoods into battlegrounds, and the innocent, then as today, were caught in the middle. Syndicates like the Chicago Outfit and the Five Families in New York became blueprints for what street empires would later become. These early street figures laid the groundwork for what would evolve into a national myth: the idea that the streets could make anyone rich and powerful overnight—but only if they were willing to risk everything.

By the 1940s and 1950s, the Great Migration brought a wave of African Americans from the rural South to northern cities, reshaping the urban landscape and introducing new elements to street culture in cities like New York, Chicago, and Los Angeles. By then, the cities were already soaked with blood and tension. The counterculture movements of the 1960s and 1970s brought more and new attention to urban struggles, setting the stage for the rise of a new type of gang culture and the underground economy fueled by the opioid and crack epidemic of the 1970s through the 1990s and even beyond.

During this time, President Richard Nixon's declaration of a "War on Drugs" collided with the rise of hip-hop. What began in the 1970s as a new form of creative expression had evolved into "gangster rap" by the 1980s. Artists like Schoolly D, Too $hort, and Ice-T began glorifying illegal activities such as drug trafficking, prostitution, and robbery while celebrating the luxurious lifestyles they claimed these acts provided. The belief that crime pays—and pays well—was amplified through their music and the media, embedding the myth even deeper into popular culture with tracks like "Dopeman" by N.W.A and films like *Scarface* and *The Godfather*.

President Ronald Reagan's continuation of the War on Drugs in the 1980s further compounded inner-city problems, as harsh drug laws targeted marginalized communities—even while his administration faced scrutiny for allowing those same drugs into America. By the 1990s, the prison population had ballooned under even stricter policies by President Bill Clinton, and vast numbers of nonviolent offenders were locked up—often for minor drug-related offenses. Adding to the injustice, the US Sentencing Commission later confirmed—and Attorney General Eric Holder publicly acknowledged—that Black male offenders received sentences that were nearly 20 percent longer than similarly situated white male offenders. This gap wasn't a coincidence but rather the product of systemic bias hidden beneath "tough on crime" policies, further exposing the lie behind the idea of easy money. These individuals and anyone caught in the War on Drugs became metaphorical prisoners of war in a conflict waged not against crime, but against the very communities it claimed to protect. The harsh realities of poverty, addiction, and systemic neglect drove crime rates even higher, while the promise of easy money in the streets came with a brutal price tag. As businessman Henry Sy once said, there is no such thing as overnight success or easy money—and the streets proved his words painfully true.

Drug dealers and those flaunting their illegal wins were often murdered for their cars, jewelry, or rims. And for many youth—whether they were criminally affiliated or not—the threat was everywhere: they could be beaten, robbed, or even killed over something as simple as a jacket or a pair of shoes.

Despite the risks, by the early 2000s, the myth persisted and had grounded itself in American society—crossing racial, social, and economic lines, especially among youth. Street culture, with its promises of power, success, and freedom, became a false fairy tale. Ambition, desperation, and greed blinded individuals to the reality that every dollar earned in the streets comes with unparalleled risks: violence, incarceration, and even death.

The truth is that street money is no easier to earn than legitimate pay. As with any business, there's only so much money to go around, and appearances can be deceiving. Just as business owners may project success while quietly surviving on credit, many on the streets do the same.

Behind the flash, countless hustlers rely on a "front"—the street's version of credit—borrowing money or drugs just to keep their heads above water. The rapper Young Buck captures this in "Plug Money," where he calls out those in street life flaunting cash that isn't even theirs. Others lean on parents, partners, or family for survival, while projecting the illusion that wealth flows easily, as if it's "all in a day's work." Eventually, many discover there's no struggle worse than being broke while trying to look rich.

Street wealth is like any form of wealth: it demands putting in relentless effort, thinking strategically, beating out rivals, adapting to changes, studying the competition, and enduring various levels of investment, sacrifice, and loss. However, street money comes with added burdens—violence, paranoia, betrayal, and the constant threat of imprisonment, or worse. What is often mistaken for easy is, in fact, the high-risk, high-stakes gamble that consumes lives and leaves most participants worse off than they began. Some sociologists, like Sudhir Venkatesh, in his work *Gang Leader for a Day: A Rogue Sociologist Takes to the Streets*, have even likened street crews to major corporations in the hood, offering risky but steady employment in places with few real options.

Ultimately, the phrase "the rewards outweigh the risks" deserves careful scrutiny and skepticism. Street life is far from a shortcut to success; more often, it is a detour leading to despair, regret, or tragedy. The harsh truth is that nothing in life is free—not even freedom, which some might argue is itself an illusion, reinforcing the natural hardships of life.

STREET VIEW

The greed surrounding street money is insatiable, making it one of the most dangerous, addictive, and unstable ways to earn a living. Yet somehow, this myth—that "street money is easy money"—not only survives but thrives. It's one of the most repeated lies ever told about street life.

People used to say to me and others, "Get a real job. Stop chasing fast and easy money," as if the hustle wasn't a job in itself. As if it didn't require the same dedication, hard work, ambition, courage, skill, and calculated risk that running a legal business does—sometimes even more. No job or business, legal or illegal, is easy to build or maintain, especially when your life or freedom is always on the line.

From the outside looking in, people make lazy assumptions. They glance at someone's life and decide they understand it. They confuse its appearance with ease. It's the same reason people think becoming a famous rapper, influencer, podcaster, investor—or even an author—is simple. The hard work is taken for granted. Street money gets thrown into that same pile of assumptions. "If they can do it, so can I." But the spectators don't know the story behind the shine: the risk in the journey, the dangers in the waters, the snakes in the tall grass. The folklore lives on.

This myth also depends on another dangerous lie: that street people aren't intelligent or strategic. They're just lucky or reckless, so the money they make must be easy. But business is business, no matter what you are selling; it's all about supply and demand.

If you enter the underworld of crime believing the myth, chances are you bring that assumption with you—and it'll likely destroy you. I've seen it happen. Assumptions have cost people their freedom, and even their lives. I, too, have paid the price for my foolish assumptions.

The less we understand something, the more gullible we become regarding it. The fame, the money, and the flashiness of the streets become a visual drug. We breathe in the aesthetic and fall into the intoxicating idea that "I can become a success overnight."

Street money is a savage business, far from easy. I had to move fast. Many sat still too long, and they didn't live long—death is not prejudiced. Over time, you become addicted to the money, the chase, the illusion of control. I never assumed street money was easy to acquire; I saw too many tragic things early on before getting any type of street money. But I became enslaved to the hustle that I did not see as a trap, an addiction. By the time you recognize it, it's probably too late. Fixations in any walk of life are usually hard to shake.

Another layer of the street money myth is the corruption around it. You come to realize the system isn't as clean as it pretends to be. You see officers in badges doing heinous things that the public rarely, if ever, hears about. You see prosecutors and public defenders play games, like "phantom court," that you've never heard of. Even judges pretend to weigh evidence against you while having already made up their minds. Then comes the betrayal, not just from the law, but from people you trust, people you'd die or kill for—who will try to kill you. And all of it, as Bone Thugs-N-Harmony or the O'Jays would say, "For the Love of Money"—or simply jealousy.

The ones who survive don't usually talk about it. They just endure quietly. They shrug and say, "It comes with the game." And even if they did speak—who would listen?

There's nothing easy about street money—on any level. It's a business, sure. But it's one with risks that most people can't stomach. It's earned in unimaginable ways, and the participants can become the monsters from your worst nightmares. Meanwhile, law enforcement is watching—waiting—salivating for your entry. Or maybe, just before the statute of limitations runs out on your crime, when you've "retired" from the game—bought a house, opened a business, and reclined with your family—it will come for you. That knock at the door will be your past life, demanding that you make amends. I've known this to happen on multiple occasions.

Worst of all, the hungry eyes of children see it and want it, some out of need, some out of curiosity. No matter the reason, all learn the hard way: street money is not a shortcut. It's a rabbit hole—hard to climb out of. It's a maze—difficult to explain. And for most, it's wiser to exhaust every moral and legal option before ever choosing that route. In many cases, patience is more valuable than the shiny objects we see.

Still, no matter the warnings, curiosity has a tendency to drown out logic. Desperation wrestles with reason. Ambition can blind you. Street money appears to offer freedom—no boss, no taxes, no time clock, no college degree, no interviews. It might give you pride, identity, respect, and even a sense of accomplishment in a world where you're finally somebody.

Eventually, it begins to feel easy, comfortable. The illusion of freedom and the aphrodisiac of power take over, and you want to keep it, expand it if possible, and protect it by any means. But freedom—on or off the streets—is an illusion. And street money sells one of the biggest illusions of all: that you answer to no one and can buy yourself out of any situation.

The truth is that the only thing that ever came easily for me pertaining to street money was how easily I misunderstood it—the rabbit hole, the addiction.

Some people argue that not all illegal money is "street money." They divide it between white-collar and blue-collar crimes—as if white-collar crime is more "prestigious." White-collar crimes are committed by professionals—bank fraud, tax evasion, money laundering, embezzlement, insider trading. Blue-collar crimes, meanwhile, are tied to the working class—pimping, drug dealing, theft, robbery. Street life.

From my view and my experience, all illegal money is street money. It all starts the same, with a need—for greed, survival, power, deception, or control. And if you're caught, it can all end the same—in prison.

In federal prisons, you can see this more clearly. Your cellmate could be your polar opposite. Someone who committed bank fraud may end up sharing a prison cell with a bank robber—or a drug dealer with an insider trader, a pimp with a cybercriminal, an embezzler with a gun runner. The law doesn't care what kind of collar you wear—just whether or not you committed a crime. Al Capone, one of the most notorious gangsters America has ever produced, wasn't taken down by his blue-collar crimes—murders, extortions, theft, or bootlegging. He was taken down by a white-collar crime—tax evasion. And the needle pierced him just the same.

While in a world of crime, I learned that street life crosses all categories. Its money reaches all locations. It exists just about everywhere—from gated communities to boarded-up housing projects. It sometimes gets washed clean and mixes itself with all other money. At that point, who can tell the difference? And who cares, anyway? With the internet and technology, all crimes are global. If it can be learned, it can be done—and street affiliates are often right in the mix.

It makes no difference whether a criminal is

- Big Meech, a drug kingpin,
- Dread Pirate Roberts, a darknet operator,
- Bernie Madoff, a financial con man,
- Bonnie Parker and Clyde Barrow, legendary armed robbers,
- Heidi Fleiss, the Hollywood Madam, or
- Sam Bankman-Fried, a crypto fraudster.

In the eyes of the system, criminals are criminals. And whether you were building a criminal empire or just trying to survive, the result is often the same.

Street money ain't easy, and if you try to "get in and get

out real quick"—make a few bucks, pay some bills, and relieve some stress—you can find yourself in a worse position than you started in. I've known people who thought financial scams were easy. The first time they stole bank profiles, slid a credit card, or wrote a check, they were in handcuffs before they knew it. Some thought robbery was easy—just wave a gun and people will comply. They wound up with a gun turned on them. Others thought going out of town to sell drugs and take over neighborhoods was just as easy as it sounded, but some came back in caskets, as Ice Cube detailed in "My Summer Vacation."

It's as simple as that. You are playing with wolves and lions. If you think you don't pay taxes—trust me, you do. Just not in installments. When you lose a shipment or the law comes knocking, you pay all at once, back taxes included.

Until then, the rewards might look like success. But no matter how it's dressed up—flashy or subtle, blue collar or white collar—street money is still an illegal acquisition of funds. And it doesn't negotiate for you. It offers no promises, no guarantees. It demands sacrifice, and often, your peace of mind. The deeper you go or the "bigger" you become, the more others will want what you have. And they'll be willing to do worse than you ever imagined to take it from you. So you either defend your position or fold to their pressure. When enough people get hurt, the impact is visible—not just in your life, but in the entire community.

This street view isn't meant to glorify or condemn—it's meant to confront. The myth is a lie. Those of us who lived through it either already knew or learned the truth the hard way.

> **THE TRUTH**
>
> There is no such thing as easy money. Life operates on goods, services, and opportunities, all of which depend on demand and supply. Not all goods or services are valuable at all times, and every opportunity carries risks, often in the face of fierce competition. Success in any venture hinges on weighing risk against reward. As the stakes get higher, the risk becomes greater and so does the potential reward, yet failure in these cases results in the hardest falls. While risks differ in severity, consequences are unavoidable—they are the cost of the gamble that life demands of us all.

STREET MONEY IS A BUSINESS.

──── **MYTH 8** ────

A PAID ATTORNEY IS ALWAYS BETTER

> Nothing in life worth having comes for free, and the higher the fee, the better the quality. When it comes to legal defense, you better know this: a paid attorney is always better. After all, you get what you pay for, and no one fights harder than someone with a high-dollar retainer on the line. Public defenders might as well be public pretenders, pretending to work for you—they're overworked, underpaid, and barely invested. But a paid attorney? That's someone who has your back. You pay them directly, so they have a personal stake in your case; their reputation depends on winning.

Street culture has long embraced the belief that hiring a paid attorney guarantees better outcomes in the criminal justice system. This myth is fueled by the assumption that money can buy anything; therefore, the more money you spend, the greater the chance of victory—whether that means reduced charges or an acquittal. Many attorneys benefit from this belief, capitalizing on the desperation of individuals who, facing life-altering accusations, are willing to pay almost any price for the hope or even an insinuated promise of freedom or leniency. As Thomas Tusser once noted, "A fool and his money are soon parted."

When public gangster figures—those who make no effort to hide their criminal status—beat high-profile cases, the myth that money buys the best defense only grows stronger. Take John Gotti, for example: famously nicknamed "the Teflon Don," he initially avoided conviction by the federal government in a jury trial, reinforcing the belief that wealth can tip the scales of justice even if you are known as an unlawful person. Though he was eventually convicted and accused of jury fixing in that first trial, his early win left a lasting impression.

The myth gained further traction in many cases. One in particular was O.J. Simpson's trial—arguably the most dissected legal battle of the twentieth century. His legal "Dream Team," which included Robert Shapiro, Johnnie Cochran, Alan Dershowitz, and Robert Kardashian (father of the now-famous Kardashian siblings), secured an acquittal for Simpson, a Black man accused of killing two white individuals. For many, this became the ultimate proof: if you can afford elite counsel, the courtroom becomes a battlefield where you can win—regardless of guilt or even prejudices.

In hip-hop culture, where street credibility often blends with celebrity influence, this belief is deeply embedded. When artists associated with street life—Snoop Dogg, Tupac Shakur, A$AP Rocky, Boosie Badazz, Gucci Mane, NBA YoungBoy, Young Thug, Hurricane Chris, and others—are found not guilty, have their charges dismissed, or receive what some call "a slap on the wrist," it strengthens the myth. Their outcomes aren't simply attributed to legal nuance—they're seen as direct results of paid power: expensive attorneys who know how to maneuver the system.

Still, the myth doesn't always hold. Suge Knight, Shyne, Tory Lanez, Remy Ma, C-Murder, and Max B are reminders that fame, fortune, and even a good attorney aren't always enough. P. Diddy's case stands as a modern example of how the myth continues to evolve. While he was found guilty on two of four charges—arguably the lesser of the four—the outcome didn't deliver a clear-cut victory or defeat. His wealth and legal team may have influenced the outcome, but they didn't erase the charges. This reminds us that sometimes a paid attorney doesn't guarantee a win, just a softer landing.

"I paid 1.3 million dollars for my attorneys, and I still got the max, 11 years."
—AN INMATE IN FEDERAL PRISON

Being accused of a crime—whether guilty or not—is a terrifying and vulnerable experience for anyone, especially for those who have little to no access to financial resources to maintain a life that's compounded with the pressures that are upon them. But individuals often equate cost with quality, believing that an expensive attorney will be more qualified, outperforming free legal counsel. While some paid attorneys are ethical and dedicated, others may exploit their clients' fears and ignorance. These attorneys may push clients to trial to feed their own egos or persuade them to sign plea deals that result in disastrous immediate and long-term consequences.

The reality is that law is a business, and like any business, profit is often the priority. The faster an attorney resolves a case, the greater their earnings per hour. This dynamic can leave clients feeling abandoned once their payment runs out, regardless of the case's outcome. Sadly, the legal system sometimes seems structured to benefit attorneys more than the public they serve. As novelist Mario Puzo once warned, lawyers with briefcases can steal more than men with guns. His warning was less about violence and more about the sanctioned power of the system that lawyers quietly but devastatingly use.

Perhaps part of that power lies in how we speak of them. The terms *lawyer* and *attorney* are often used interchangeably, especially in everyday conversation, and in many contexts they generally mean the same thing. However, there is a subtle but important distinction between the two. A lawyer has a law degree and can offer legal advice or draft documents. An attorney is a lawyer who has also passed the bar exam and is licensed to represent clients in court. So all attorneys are lawyers—but not all lawyers are attorneys.

Historically, the legal profession has evolved from ancient Greek orators and Roman jurisconsults to the structured legal advocacy we see today. By the medieval period, legal education and professional ethics had become central to the practice of law, cementing its role as a necessary institution for navigating complex legal systems. While the profession has developed significantly, its accessibility and fairness remain points of contention.

Still, it is crucial to recognize that free counsel, such as public defenders or pro bono lawyers, often provide representation that rivals or surpasses that of paid counsel. Public defenders and pro bono attorneys are typically skilled and experienced, handling a high volume of cases with an intimate understanding of the system. This is not to claim that free representation is always better or worse than paid counsel but to challenge the assumption that money guarantees superior legal defense.

Ultimately, the best defense comes from being informed. If accused of a crime, you should research your case thoroughly; understand the charges, the proceedings, and the language; and evaluate the attorneys that are available, paid or otherwise. Above all, avoid the misconception that any attorney, paid or free, can "save" you from the consequences of any accusation. The justice system is inherently unpredictable; other players (judges, prosecutors, juries) are involved, and no particular representation can guarantee a specific outcome.

As a judge once told me, "I'm not bound by anything that's written in this plea agreement. I can give you whatever sentence I want."

STREET VIEW

Before I ever stepped into street life, I was just an inner-city kid. Every so often I would listen to the grown-ups speak on the "greatness" of having a lawyer in your life. Paid attorneys were spoken of like superheroes. But in the world of blue-collar and white-collar criminals, they were legends—part savior, part status symbol. "Keep bail money and have an attorney on retainer," was the common advice passed around like gospel. Even my own mother once told one of my older brothers, "I don't know how you're getting all this money, but I'm sure you're doing something you shouldn't. So go and retain an attorney." But I learned through experience that the devil is in the details, and money can't always get someone out of trouble. Sometimes it only buys disappointment and prolongs the problem.

I came up in the eighties and nineties—an era where TV, movies, and pop culture made lawyers look like rock stars. They were shown as smooth-talking, briefcase-carrying masterminds who could dismantle the courtroom with a few words and a sharp suit. They were almost always white or Jewish, portrayed as brilliant and charismatic, and usually second only to doctors or scientists in intelligence, or to preachers in moral clout. Female attorneys were seen as even more dangerous and fascinating—beautiful, articulate, and ruthless in heels.

What fascinated me most was how lawyers seemed to navigate both sides of the law. One day they'd be locking up drug lords as prosecutors; the next day, they'd be opening up their own law firms as defense attorneys, freeing the same criminals for six figures or more a case. The hypocrisy was obvious even then. Still, society held them in high regard. So as a kid, I bought into it like everyone else: if you can afford a paid attorney, you'll be all right.

Like most street dudes, I started off small-time—petty crimes and impulsive decisions. I was patient in my growth, saving money for my own "slick-talking white lawyer." And when the time came, I could fight in the "big times." Until then, I settled for public defenders. Looking back, that wasn't always a bad thing. It saved me money and spared me the disillusionment of thinking I could buy my way out of the consequences with some golden-ticket lawyer like I was Charlie in *Willy Wonka*.

In the streets, we all knew someone or were that someone who got arrested. When the money got low and the case got real, everybody started scrambling, calling friends and family to "chip in on an attorney." But truth be told, in many of those cases, spending money on a paid attorney only made things worse. I saw it happen, again and again, as I put my money in the hands of those who I assumed were saving our family or friends from the inevitable.

Some attorneys had egos bigger than their skillsets. They

seemed sadistic, convincing my friends to sign plea deals they'd regret for life. Others pushed them to trial, talking about how they could "beat the case," but in reality they were just trying to show off their courtroom theatrics—only to lose, badly. Friends and family were sentenced for their entire lives. We used to call those outcomes "football numbers." And even after these disasters, the attorneys always had some slick excuse and were ready to move on to their next paying client, untouched and unfazed.

That's when I started to question what attorneys really were. Were they professionals? Performers? Parasites? Were they there to defend the accused or to feast on their desperation and fear?

When you grow up hearing that a paid lawyer is better, your mind tries to hold on to that hope, that conditioning. You think, *Maybe I just didn't pay enough. Maybe if I hire the right one, it'll be different.* That kind of thinking is dangerous because it's not based on law; it's based on myth.

I found that out on a more personal level, in a very hard way, when I graduated from local jails and state prisons to a federal indictment. That's when shit got real.

The federal system isn't just different—it's a monster. To put it bluntly, I knew I'd fucked up. This was a whole new world of legal problems. In spite of all my assumptions, I finally saw I wasn't prepared for it. My state attorneys didn't have the eligibility to represent me in a federal case, and I quickly learned that the feds don't play by the same rules, and everything was different.

Still, while I was locked in a cage, chained from wrist to waist to ankles, I met many blue-collar and white-collar criminals who had put their hopes and lives in the hands of expensive or inexpensive federal attorneys. "Save your money. A lawyer is not going to help you here," they would all say.

Surprisingly, even a bald-headed, tattooed white supremacist tried to warn me of this. I ignored him, of course. I judged the messenger and missed the message, partially because I didn't believe the horror stories. *It can't be that bad,* I thought. I needed something that was going to comfort me in my moment of grief. "What are attorneys for?" I held on to the myth, the fairy tale that my money would fight for me. But heartbreakingly, some games have to be played all the way to the end.

When they're working on drug cases, the feds don't "make deals"; they only make rats. So either rat on your friends or be prepared for a federal tribunal.

Some attorneys—federal or state—have an ethical code. They don't help clients become rats. They'll say, "If you ever decide to go down that path, you need to find new counsel because I don't fuck with rats." Why this was, I never found out. But I respected the lines they wouldn't cross as some respected that I wouldn't cross that line either.

Still, the federal system was worse than the state system. Lawyers charged more but had a lower chance of getting positive results. I eventually learned that I needed to start reading case law and diligently study my own case to understand the "legal jargon" spoken in or out of the courtroom.

That was when I really saw the game: many lawyers speak with a forked tongue. They say they represent you, but they're often working with the system to prosecute you—bleeding you for information. Some don't care to fight; they see you as a lost cause, an easy check. And if you don't know the law yourself, you'll spot their antics.

I went through attorney after attorney. Some tried to pressure me to cooperate with the government. One actually told the judge I was guilty and I wasn't a small-time drug dealer, standing on the corners selling nickels and dimes, so he could trust that I wouldn't go back to selling if I was let out on bond. Others were lazy, pushing pleas in my face without reviewing a single page of discovery. A few were outright liars, telling me things I knew weren't true—because I'd started studying my own case and researching case law. The more you know, the more you will understand who is trying to fuck you and who is trying to help you.

The money I spent was gone—tens of thousands I'd never get back. And in the end, after two and a half years of fighting, I pleaded guilty to conspiracy to distribute ten thousand ecstasy pills. My attorney showed me an email from the judge that I'd be sentenced to five to six years, based on my pre-sentence investigation report. But I warned her that wouldn't happen—the judge had already made up his mind during the evidentiary hearing, and the email he sent her was a farce. She called me cynical and claimed I was wrong and would soon see. Almost two months later, I was sentenced to nine years in federal prison and three years of supervised release—not because of what my lawyer did or didn't do, but because that's what the system was always going to give me anyways.

So, yes, "save your money" turned out to be the right strategy, at least in my case.

Nevertheless, I learned a lot through my experience with both paid and unpaid attorneys, state and federal. Some people will say, "The real lesson is that you shouldn't have been committing crimes to begin with," while others will advise you, "Only pay a lawyer if you're going to trial—everything else is just a performance." I won't argue with either. Neither is totally true, but there's some truth in both, I'm sure. But the biggest truth I learned was this:

Paying for an attorney doesn't guarantee honesty.

It doesn't guarantee power.

It doesn't guarantee freedom.

No matter how prestigious an attorney may seem or who recommends them, they don't automatically come with a "get out of jail free" card.

I've seen public defenders fight harder than paid attorneys and paid lawyers do a worse job than court-appointed ones. I've seen money buy hope—and nothing else. People with no law degree who decided to represent themselves have effectively won their own cases.

At the end of the day, if your lawyer, paid or unpaid, doesn't bring integrity, skill, and real effort to the table, you become a lost cause. In many cases, even if they do these things, it's still not enough.

And worst of all? Judges don't care how much you spent. No amount of money will protect you from a judge who's already made up their mind. Judges—not the Constitution, not the law, not the prosecutor, and not your attorney—get the final word. Just them. They can bend the rules, write anything in their "opinions," say whatever they want in their rulings, reinterpret evidence, or deliver a sentence based on how they feel that day. If you appeal their ruling, as I did, this will just land you in front of another judge or judges who hold the same power. And your high-paid attorney? They will do what you are told to do: wait. And the cycle repeats.

THE TRUTH

Not all things with a price tag are worth what they cost. "Free" is sometimes a blessing. In all courtrooms, the ultimate decider in a case is a judge, not the attorney you hired. If a judge concludes that, for whatever reason, someone should go free, then that is what will happen. If the judge sentences someone to prison, that will be their destiny. Good, bad, or indifferent, that is the simple truth. Even if the judgment is argued up the ladder to higher courts, the ultimate decider is still a judge and not the attorney you hired.

A PAID ATTORNEY ISN'T ALWAYS BETTER.

MYTH 9

IT'S MORE GANGSTER TO GO FED THAN STATE

> To catch the attention of the federal government, you have to be a major player in the game—deeply connected or involved in crimes that shake the foundation of society. The feds don't waste their time on small-time hustlers; they only go after those seen as the biggest threats, the ones making the most noise or moving enough weight. Facing federal rather than state charges is proof that your moves were gangster and big enough to get on the radar of the most powerful law enforcement in the country.

In street lore, federal prison time has its own mystique: inmates are locked away and treated like celebrity prisoners, and these prisons are rumored to be cushier than state lockups. The myth whispers that going federal is a badge of honor—proof that you were big enough, destructive enough, or smart enough for the feds to go after you. It says that you were running top-tier operations, earning the ultimate gangster stripes, or you and your team were the ultimate threat to society at large. You, as a prisoner, are imagined to be in the same league as those seen in movies, heard about in rap lyrics, or read about in books and magazines.

But in the unforgiving world of street life, myths often distort reality, creating fantasies that entice while obscuring truths and harsh consequences. This myth, deeply embedded across generations, holds the belief that it's "more gangster" to serve time in a federal prison than in a state prison. This mindset glorifies incarceration, ignoring the psychological, emotional, and societal costs that come with it. As Bertrand Russell once observed, "One should respect public opinion only enough to avoid starvation and prison—anything more is surrendering to an unnecessary tyranny." Yet in the streets, this so-called tyranny is embraced, even sought after, as if a federal sentence were a badge of honor rather than a chain of bondage.

As Larry Hoover (the founder of Chicago's Gangster Disciples) described—or warned—in a letter to the public from a federal supermax prison in 2022, "The immediate and enduring consequence I have suffered is to have been confined within the ADX Colorado. This facility is often depicted and characterized as the 'Alcatraz of the Rockies' or, as one prior Warden has said, 'It's as close to Hell as possible.' I can tell you that after 25 years within this place, these are apt descriptions."

Isolation, solitary confinement, and the brutal routines of "correctional" facilities often leave individuals institutionalized or battling mental illnesses like depression and anxiety. You can enter prison as a nonviolent offender, but because of the constant exposure to violence—and sometimes the need to adapt just to survive—you can easily come out hardened, aggressive, and mentally and emotionally scarred. The forced adaptation to a violent environment changes people, often for the worse. This kind of torment exists at the state and federal levels of incarceration. Even the late Stanley "Tookie" Williams, co-founder of the Crips, described state prison life in *Blue Rage, Black Redemption* as a volatile and unpredictable world—where today's friend can become tomorrow's number one enemy and violence can erupt without warning. That kind of instability leaves deep psychological wounds that linger long after a sentence is over.

Despite these realities, this myth persists, amplified by entertainment and social media, which idolize figures like John Gotti, Freeway Ricky, El Chapo, Big Meech, and Larry Hoover. These names and many others are celebrated in songs, movies, and street lore as icons of power and status, while their regrets or ultimate fates are either downplayed or ignored entirely. Some of these figures have spoken out against the life they once embodied, expressing regret and warning others of its dangers. Others, like John Gotti, accepted all that they had done with no regret, expressing this via Bruce Cutler: "I am me. I ain't gonna change. The people who love me will love me until I die. The rest? That's their business."

The harshness of street life convinces many young boys that they aren't truly "solidified" unless they can survive jail or prison. To prove themselves, they embrace the prospect of incarceration as a test—walking the yards, holding their heads high, repping their hoods, fighting at the slightest provocation, even killing if called upon. In this way, prison becomes a rite of passage, redefining how manhood is measured in the streets—and tragically, in life more broadly. This mindset is reinforced in the very culture they consume: Snoop Dogg's "Murder Was the Case" frames prison as an inevitable consequence, Kurupt's "Behind the Walls" paints the daily reality of incarceration, Pooh Shiesty's "Federal Contraband 2" brings light to the hustle behind bars, and Ludacris's "Do Your Time" (featuring Beanie Sigel, Pimp C, and C-Murder) speaks of serving a bid as a sign of strength and honor. The music doesn't just reflect the streets—it fuels the belief that prison is both the proving ground and the price of manhood.

This belief intensifies when the conversation turns to federal prisons. Dating as far back as Alcatraz—home to America's most infamous criminals, like Al Capone, Machine Gun Kelly, Whitey Bulger, Frank Morris, and "Bumpy" Johnson—federal time has been portrayed as a badge reserved for elite offenders. Linking federal time with wealth, intelligence, and notoriety creates a dangerous narrative: that survival in federal confinement elevates your rank in the unspoken hierarchy of street life, reinforcing the idea that only the greatest warriors are worthy of the greatest force to bring them down.

This myth also feeds into the assumption—or myth—that federal agencies must or will watch individuals for months or even years before making an arrest or that only those deeply entrenched in major crimes—like trafficking large quantities of drugs—fall under federal scrutiny. However, evidence repeatedly shows that federal authorities can be just as "petty" as local police departments, charging individuals for minor offenses, including possession of small amounts of drugs.

This reality shatters the illusion of federal prison as an exclusive club reserved for "big-time gangsters" and "big-time drug dealers" and exposes the myth for what it truly is: a dangerous and deceptive narrative that elevates incarceration while ignoring its true cost.

Yet the supposed prestige of federal incarceration persists. While federal facilities are often perceived as having better living conditions than state prisons, they are no less harsh. Furthermore, federal sentences are often harsher than state ones for the same crimes, ensuring longer terms of confinement and greater disruption to the lives of those who are incarcerated and their families.

Prisons themselves have evolved from what was supposed to have been tools of rehabilitation and deterrence to engines of profiteering and a breeding ground for even more dangerous people. Federal Bureau of Prisons (BOP) budgets have been cut over time, even into the present, curtailing all the "amenities," or what could be seen as luxury items, for which federal prisons are widely known.

Today they are an industrial complex where human lives are commodified for labor, funding, and profit. This reality starkly contrasts the myth of honor and status, revealing incarceration as a mechanism of control that benefits privately owned prisons and jail systems, stock companies, and political power—not individuals who may truly need help.

The system is its own worst enemy—built by people shaped by its dysfunction. It creates problems just to profit politically or financially from fixing them.

STREET VIEW

By the time I was twelve years old, in 1987, the myth that "it's more gangster to go fed than state" was already starting to consume me. I was at an impressionable age, and the streets—the people, the energy, the mystique—were pulling me in, moment by moment, bit by bit, year after year.

I was spoon-fed the lie by people I looked up to. They, too, had been consumed by the myth. They'd say, "If you're gonna commit a crime and end up in prison, go federal. That's where the real gangstas at. At least you live better." I held on to those words like gospel. They shaped my thinking, influenced my decisions, and made federal time sound like a badge of honor. I began to see it as the proof of my hustle, my hate for the system, even my hate for life, wrapped up in one destiny: federal prison.

Even earlier than that, by the time I was ten, I had already begun to equate "gangster" with manhood. Like most kids, I trusted the people I could see, talk to, and be around. My idols weren't on TV; they were in the neighborhoods I lived in. They were the people gangster rappers talked about and, most of all, pretended to be. They didn't just tell me how to live in the streets—they showed me. "Never snitch. Go to prison. Do your time. Don't let nobody play you. Come home and get back in the game." That was the cycle. That was the code. And it started to seem like the norm.

I learned early on that when you walk into any jail or prison, you walk in with your head up. No matter how short you are. No matter if it's your first time in. Stand on who you are. Be you—nothing more. That's what will carry you. Don't fake it. Fight and die for the man you are in your heart and not the man anyone else expects you to be.

Before I was locked up, I remember how Polaroid pictures from state prisons were sent home like trophies, showing off the "gangster look": flexed muscles, serious posture, proud stares next to comrades. These were known as "prison poses." They made incarceration look honorable, like a rite of passage, something to be proud of.

In our young minds, we began to brand ourselves with the idea that this could be us someday. And for many, it was. Quietly, subconsciously, we internalized the future.

Back then, going to state prison was more common. But whispers of going federal were on the lips of many. Rumors floated that you had to be "big time" to make it there. You had to be a major player in a major conspiracy for the feds to be interested in you. Naturally, that boosted the myth, elevated the expectations, and distorted the idea of what it meant to be a "real" gangster.

Hollywood and the media outlets helped too. Movies were showing the CIA's large-scale operations, and news reports sensationalized federal takedowns. The FBI, DEA, CIA, and ATF became part of the legend. "The feds only go after the elite," we thought. "Petty criminals? Nah, they don't waste their time." So the myth kept growing.

State prisons were known for violent offenders, unstable personalities, and chaotic energy. But federal? That was different. That's where the legends were—mob bosses, cartel leaders, hitmen, hackers, CEOs, scammers, the powerful, the legends. These weren't just criminals; they were dignified villains who were feared and respected. Their reputations elevated the myth even more.

Stories floated around about "country club" prisons—feds with swimming pools, tennis courts, better food. Very few of us could say firsthand, "Yeah, I got family in the feds."

By 1988, my own brother—a drug dealer, a gangster—who had already done time in state prison, was taken down by the federal government, once widely known as "the long arm of the law." This arrest, for him, for all of us, was different from the earlier ones. It was painful, yes. But in our world, it was seen as just part of the game.

By 1993, things intensified for many more families. The Crime Bill—written by Joe Biden and cosigned by politicians of all backgrounds—was signed into law by President Bill Clinton. It intensified the already exploding federal prison population, enforcing draconian sentences that didn't just punish people, but destroyed minority families and sent their communities into chaos. And the myth? It kept growing. Each generation passed it on, some with fear, others with pride.

Prior to this, in 1987, President Ronald Regan had been under scrutiny because officials in his administration were said to be involved in allowing vast amounts of drugs into America; this would later be known as the Contra scandal. Still, Congress enacted additional, harsher laws to arrest people, especially minorities, for possessing the very drugs government officials were suspected of allowing to come into the country. At this point, federal arrests became more common in Black and Brown communities, and the prison population exploded with minor drug offenders and low-level criminals.

In time, nearly everyone knew someone who had been to federal prison. And if you yourself had been? It became part of your street résumé in a culture lit on fire by a myth. Rap music poured gasoline on the flames. Lines about beating federal cases or getting indicted by "the alphabet boys" turned into street anthems. The FBI, DEA, ATF—even the CIA—became characters in this bizarre drama, mythologized as much as the criminals themselves were.

Women began to directly or indirectly brag about having men in the feds. State prison was serious too, but for most, their man being in federal lockup increased their own social value. Saying, "My nigga in the feds," would prompt others to pause, stare, and ask, "Why he in the feds?" Children and parents also began to wear the affiliation like a badge. Proof in point, even Martha Stewart herself got some "street cred" for doing a few months in a fed camp. It was no longer something to be ashamed of. The message was everywhere: fight the feds, beat the feds, be in the feds—you're different now. You're validated.

But behind the myth, the truth was darker. Many gangsters feared the feds; they didn't toy with that reality. Even the

Notorious B.I.G. reiterated this in the song "You're Nobody (Til Somebody Kills You)." They already knew how hard-hitting they were; others did not. Many didn't believe they were "fedworthy," so they continued in what they assumed were local and state crimes until they found out the hard way that the alphabet boys no longer reserved their reach for legends. The truth is that, over time, they lowered their standards. What was once seen as an exclusive pursuit of high-profile criminals became a sweeping dragnet for anyone and anything. The same charge that might get probation in state court could land you five to thirty years in the feds. Petty crimes, first-time offenses, and old charges you already served time for—all could be weaponized under federal sentencing laws.

Mandatory minimums. Career criminal enhancements. Sentences that made no logical sense. The feds had evolved from elite enforcers to a supercharged police department with unlimited resources and unchecked power, thanks to the men and women in power cosigning and sponsoring bills. I guess it's true that "the pen is mightier than the sword."

But the myth? It didn't care. The myth turned federal time into a stripe on your jacket instead of a scar on your life. The myth made it sound like a reward, not a consequence. It glorified having your name attached to a prison sentence but ignored the trauma, the isolation, the lost years, the broken relationships, the mental toll, the people who forget you, the ones who leave, and the person you become after being buried alive in a cage of steel and concrete. All the streets will say is "he'll be all right."

With experience, I began to see things differently. Those who fed me that myth were just as lost as I was. I had been raised by the streets and conditioned by a lie. But a myth can't comfort you in a cold cell. It won't protect you from regret. It just leaves you there, alone, to figure out a new way to survive.

And the streets? They move on. Fast. You get replaced more quickly than you'd think—by someone more reckless, more ambitious, or more foolish. Your name might live on in stories or, more likely, it will get lost in the pages of street history. Either way, the game keeps spinning. You are expendable.

There are bigger goals in life than making any level of prison—federal or state—a part of your identity. But if that's your goal, no one can argue with you. We all choose our paths; not everyone agrees. Just ask yourself, "What comes after that?" If the myth convinces you that a prison cell is your badge of honor, your validation, your final destination, then maybe an open heart and some open-minded therapy should come first.

> **THE TRUTH**
>
> Federal law enforcement is nothing more than a common police force with unlimited resources and a seemingly dignified presentation. They are known to arrest and lock away minor drug offenders and brand them as "career criminals." So "going fed" doesn't make someone more gangster; it just means the consequences for that individual are more severe, even for the smallest act. And being locked away in any facility will shape someone, for better or for worse.

IT'S MORE GANGSTER TO EDUCATE YOURSELF BEFORE IT'S TOO LATE.

MYTH 10

ONCE SOLID, ALWAYS SOLID

> Once a person is solid, you have their guarantee—a bond as dependable as steel and unyielding in the face of adversity. Their loyalty and principles become a currency you can bank on, a level of reliability that cannot be forfeited or withdrawn; it's simply who they are. They are the foundation of trust, the embodiment of integrity. It is impossible for them to fold or falter, no matter how heavy the weight placed upon them. Their track record speaks for itself—resilience under fire, an unshakable stance against pressures that would break any other.

Street life has long perpetuated the belief that once you've proved your loyalty, that loyalty is eternal and unwavering. This optimism, in a world defined by treachery and a few shifting rules, is remarkable but dangerously naive. In a lifestyle that demands so much in so little time, the stakes are high, and the standards for trust can seem surprisingly low. Yet this belief persists, even though the reality often proves far more unpredictable.

History—inside and outside street life—teaches us that self-preservation often trumps loyalty. Take the rapper Lil Durk, for example: he remains in custody on murder-for-hire charges, allegedly implicated by a member of his own group, Only the Family (OTF), who cooperated with authorities over several years by wearing a wire. Despite such betrayals, many in street life—be they newcomers, family, old friends, or intimate partners—cling to the belief that once you're "solid," you'll always remain so. In most cases, this gamble ends in heartbreak, incarceration, or even death, leaving many to wonder, as Tupac did, "Why U Turn on Me?"

Trust is a fundamental human need, and progress in any lifestyle requires it. But in the fast-paced world of street life, trust is often extended too quickly, particularly by the easily led and inexperienced members.

In street life, the trust of the innocent is often bought, sold, or stolen by those who are artful in the work of lies and deceit. Those seeking companionship, validation, or quick rewards often place their trust in people who haven't earned it. These rushed connections create fragile alliances, built more on need than on truth. Trust is rare and easily abused. As rapper Eminem once reflected, in a world where loyalty is uncertain and betrayal is common, trust is too precious to give away freely—so he keeps his circles small and approaches new friendships with caution. In environments like this, where trust must be earned and guarded, the term *solid* takes on a deeper meaning. It becomes a badge of honor. It says you are unbreakable, tested by past challenges, and deemed trustworthy and dependable. Being solid—or "stand-up," "A1 since day one," or "100"—is associated with integrity, strength, and loyalty, which leads many to utter phrases like "That's my nigga, so I know he solid." But the danger lies in assuming that past actions guarantee future behavior. In a world where survival is paramount, circumstances—and people—can change as swiftly as the weather, and soon enemies become friends and friends become enemies.

People are not static; we are fluid, constantly evolving as we navigate new challenges, ideas, and priorities. This inherent human adaptability is what makes the myth of "once solid, always solid" so dangerous. While someone may be steadfast today, they are not immune to shifting perspectives or pressures tomorrow.

Yet the allure of this myth persists, fueled by the longing for the perfect ally who will stand unwaveringly by one's side, through right or wrong. The quest for someone to embody this ideal often leads to disillusionment, as very few have proven to live up to certain expectations and the inflexible character of always being the same person forever.

In the end, many have stood on their word and remained solid, but the belief in "once solid, always solid" is a gamble with high stakes—a myth that overlooks the fluid, ever-changing nature of human behavior in the face of survival, opportunity, and self-preservation.

STREET VIEW

Street life—once famously known as the underworld—is like any other world. It has its systems, routines, and complex rules. It runs on many moving parts, predictable in some ways, wildly unpredictable in others. It's unstable, dangerous, and difficult to navigate. But through it all, you're expected to remain one thing: solid.

My greatest pride in street life was being solid. For me, that was worth more than money. Sticking to the code was my personal proof of who I was, the measure of my identity. Because of that, I never learned or mastered one of the oldest and most useful tricks in street life, or in life in general: pretending. I've seen plenty of people master this: acting phony to get what they want by attaining false friendships, hugging their enemies, avoiding confrontations with a smile, and getting a leg up on others. But fake handshakes and fraudulent smiles just weren't in my character. To me, those things were a contradiction of what the code was supposed to stand for. You couldn't be solid if you were pretending with people, I thought. I later realized that it's an art form—Machiavellian even. If you can pull it off—and the vast majority do—you're undoubtedly ahead of the game. That is the reality among many.

People hope and even demand that you will be solid, unshakable, dependable. Some people—naively or just desperately—bet their lives on your ability to be just that.

But being solid? Isn't easy.

The word rolls off the tongue smoothly. Makes you feel proud and cool, like you're built differently. But the reality? The road is rough—especially when the people around you aren't walking it the same. Staying solid takes mental conditioning, inner discipline, lived experience, and sometimes a specific kind of upbringing. It takes sacrifice. It takes work, street smarts. It's a job that requires you to put on blinders and walk a narrow path. One mistake, one misstep, can cost you, and even those around you, everything.

Most newcomers walk into street life thinking they'll be solid forever. They'll be loyal to the code, steady under pressure, the one people can count on. They believe their loyalty is unbreakable, their strength unmatched. They think they can stand tall in the face of betrayal, fear, law enforcement, or even death. Their ambition outweighs their understanding or their full concept of street life. They repeat "pressure makes diamonds," but forget that it also bursts pipes.

I've seen some of the most respected street figures crack under that pressure. And when they do, it's not just reputations that shatter; it's codes, relationships, and entire realities. Empires crumble. Men turn into whimpering boys, begging for the simple things they took for granted.

In street life, *solid* had a meaning that varied from person to person. Like the G Code, it was rooted in shared principles, but being solid was more personal. You lived your own definition through your actions. In short, being solid meant you had proven you could live up to the G Code. Once you did, you were stamped—solidified.

That's why it was one of the street's sacred words, revered like *respect* and rooted deep in the culture.

To be solid meant you'd been put through many strenuous tests and proved you wouldn't fold under pressure. You never snitched, even when decades of prison were staring you in the face, and you fought the pressure to switch sides when easier options appeared. That was when your name was supposed to be etched in stone—solid.

But at some point, the word *solid* became loosely used and loosely defined. Everyone was solid. The weak were stamping the weak as solid without the test that was meant to establish them. The vigorous challenges became frail, feeble. They were simple things like selling some drugs, beating up a few people, having tattoos on the face, smoking weed together, looking muscular, talking the loudest, becoming famous, or handing out a few bucks. Doing any of these could allow you to become part of a league that wore a jersey with "solid" on the back.

Being solid, when done right, often requires silence, humility. It means saying nothing, even when you know your kids are about to grow up without you, the person you love will eventually share your bed with someone else, or someone in your family is dying and you won't be there to comfort those who need it—even when it breaks your heart. You eat it. That's the part no one brags about: you do it all quietly.

That's when integrity comes into play—when no one else can see you. How do you judge yourself when nobody's looking, when the room is empty, when you're all alone and the mask comes off? That's the core solid—not the performance, not the show, but the part of you that suffers in silence, that answers to the man in the mirror. Everything else is a facade because that's what street reputations are built on: a show, a perception. Gangsters do gangster shit...until they don't.

But even the most battle-tested names fall. Look at John Gotti. He believed Sammy the Bull was solid. Sammy had proven himself, over and over. But eventually something cracked. Sammy flipped. He became the very thing everyone believed he'd never be: a rat.

That's where the moral tug-of-war begins and a contradictory life is created.

Sammy isn't the only one. Across cities and countries, gangsters and street figures who once ran empires have crawled into the hands of governments they hated, only to become informants, snitches, cooperators—the very people they once ridiculed, despised, and even killed.

In the streets, being known as solid makes people trust you. They'll do business with you, go to war for you, let you in their homes, and trust you with their lives. It helps the chaos feel manageable. But past behavior doesn't guarantee future actions. Just because someone was solid yesterday doesn't mean they'll be solid tomorrow. And just because they were solid with someone else doesn't mean they'll be solid with you.

I have many experiences to prove this reality; sadly, I had to learn the hard way.

On May 26, 2010, I was indicted by the federal government alongside two other men. We were charged with conspiracy to distribute ten thousand pills of ecstasy—MDMA or MDA.

What followed wasn't just a legal battle; it was a collapse of everything I thought I knew: about the code, loyalty, brotherhood, and what it really means to be solid.

One of my co-defendants—a man with a "solid" history—ended up folding. He checked every box: prior time served, respected crew, gang ties, solid yard time, all of it. We knew each other's people. But a few weeks in, my lawyer brought me a statement—his statement—in black and white, implicating me.

Even worse, and more disappointing, he snitched to his local police, not realizing they had already been working with the feds for months to take him down. One of his phones was tapped, and he was under home surveillance long before he ever made that statement. When he eventually found out it was a federal case, he panicked and tried to withdraw what he said about me.

All that "solid" he claimed to stand on meant nothing the moment he thought he could speak casually to the neighborhood officers he'd known for years—thinking it would stay between them. Of course, all of that was later confirmed in my federal paperwork.

That moment became my moment, like others before me. It's the moment that gangsters and street affiliates dread—being ratted out by someone you thought was solid. It was my wake-up call. I had been through it before—being ratted out—but this time it hit differently. This time, I thought I knew the man. I believed in the myth. Like the streets would say, I fell for the "okie doke." And as the song goes, "Everybody Plays the

Fool." That day, I was Boo Boo the Fool—played, manipulated, and given my dose of reality.

The local police had already arrested me before he ratted me out. Even though the feds instructed the police department to "only pull him over and identify the driver because we aren't sure if he has anything to do with any of this, we'll find out about him later," the PD disobeyed the direct order, and I was profiled, pulled over, and arrested without cause. Then they went to search for evidence to hold me indefinitely. So his snitching was just insult added to injury, but it was still snitching.

I stood tall and took the fall. As the "supplier," I was sentenced to nine years in federal prison and three years of supervised release. I went down with the ship, just as the code expects you to.

Even though it cost me almost everything, there was still something in me that felt proud to have stood solid, with no regrets.

But don't get it twisted.

Prison is no reward. There's no fanfare. No applause. You still are forced to fight for your life, even among other so-called solid men. It's a never-ending battle. And when you come home, people have moved on. The world doesn't pause for you. And most of the street dudes who once claimed they would never bow to the system and would always be solid? They've started proudly working jobs, raising families, paying taxes, and becoming part of that very system they once claimed to stand against. Like the old saying goes, if you can't beat 'em, join 'em.

There are no Purple Hearts for being solid. There are no pensions, no benefits, no Social Security, no SSI, and no 401(k)s—just stories told by the ones who made it through. There are scars you carry, pain you don't speak about, pride in your chest that sometimes feels more like a weight than an honor, and confusion you have to work through—usually alone.

After knowing all this, you still gamble on the hope that others will be solid. And they gamble that you will be too, because loyalty is currency in the streets. It buys trust, swaps for respect, makes money, moves product, and builds empires outside the law. And we all want to believe it too. We hope that loyalty and strength have no expiration date, are timeless. We want characters to be bulletproof. We want to believe toughness is Teflon.

And if it is not, then late at night, when it's quiet and no one's around, you may ask yourself a question nobody else can answer:

Was it even worth it?

THE TRUTH

People aren't meant to stay the same forever. For better or worse, we all change. And whoever's on the receiving end of that change will feel its effects, whether it brings out their better angels or their worst. It's a person's prerogative to change their mind, with or without warning—and they can and will do so whenever they see fit. Many of us have paid a price, and many more will continue to do so when they assume they know someone. Every one of us is either a benefactor or a victim of someone else's change, no matter what that change is.

THINGS THAT SEEM SOLID CAN CHANGE.

MYTH 11

FAMILY IS ALWAYS LOYAL

> Blood is thicker than water. Me and my people are one. Family sticks together—no street code or rival can break us. Family loyalty is inherited, not earned. Our shared history runs deeper; the family tree roots are strong—stronger than the G Code itself—and hold firmer than anything else in this world.

"Family is always loyal": these words offer a comforting assurance that very few would challenge. In a world of chaos and crime, people grasp for any semblance of stability, and the concept of unwavering family loyalty often becomes a beacon. But no matter how reassuring this idea may seem, it is ultimately a myth. This myth implies a bond so resilient that it will endure every test—betrayal, hardship, greed, or survival. In the perilous world of street life, however, where even the strongest individuals can be broken, this fairy tale often falls short. Loyalty is far more complex than the ties of blood, childhood memories, or a shared family name. When the stakes involve freedom, wealth, or survival, family bonds are tested in ways that expose the cracks: cousins become adversaries, siblings turn into strangers, and even the sacred ties between parents and children can fracture. This is often people's greatest heartbreak.

Since the beginning of time, family has been viewed as the cornerstone of survival—a safe haven, a source of identity, and often the foundation for one's success. As author Jane Howard once noted, whether you call it a clan, a network, or a tribe, everyone needs a family in some form to make it through life.

In street life, these ideals are relentlessly challenged by a harsh reality—loyalty is not guaranteed by birthright, nor is it an immutable truth. The streets operate on a different logic, where the mantras "every man for himself" and "trust no one" reign supreme. In such an environment, and in many parts of life in general, deception becomes second nature, and familial loyalty is stripped of its romanticized aura, often rotting like fruit left too long in the sun.

When loyalty among family members breaks down, it often becomes a one-way highway—one person driving in the darkest hours, waiting in vain for others to join the journey. Still, the myth persists, drawing strength from sayings like "blood is thicker than water." Yet history and experience prove that loyalty within families can be pawned off for personal gain. The quest for street fame, notoriety, or mere survival erodes the bonds we assume are indestructible. Family becomes a name, a label stripped of its meaning and pawned off in the pursuit of individual ambition.

"Every man looks out for himself, and he has the happiest life who manages to hoodwink himself best of all."

—FYODOR DOSTOEVSKY

The idea of family loyalty, once a pillar of strength, can transform into a dangerous liability. It fosters complacency, lulling individuals into trusting people whose priorities lie elsewhere. Loyalty, whether familial or otherwise, must be earned and constantly maintained. It is not an unshakable birthright; it is a fragile, conditional agreement that can be betrayed with little or no pressure.

In the dangerous terrain of street life, blind faith in familial loyalty can lead to ruin. The painful truth is that family, for many, becomes a concept untethered from reality—a tradition assumed but rarely fulfilled. As the bonds erode, those who cling to the myth of loyalty often find themselves isolated, burdened with disappointment, and left to navigate the journey alone.

STREET VIEW

Ever since I was a child, my immediate family—my brothers and sisters—were rarely close. Beyond them, there was the extended family: cousins, aunties, uncles, and grandparents. I was raised to believe that the word *family* was sacred—the highest of titles. I had an innate desire to belong, so naturally, in my innocence, I welcomed them all. I assumed that family loyalty, even when tested by the streets, could never be broken, especially when other family members had adopted the street code themselves.

But over time, I learned that both the code and the bond of family—no matter how strong you think it is—will get tested in the school of hard knocks. Greed, unresolved trauma, competition, jealousy, deep-seated hate, or misplaced loyalty can expose how watered down some blood ties can be, and those families who aren't strong and stable will fail and succumb to the myth. This is what happened to me.

In the life of crime, I believed my first duty was to my family members who lived the same life of crime that I did. I believed the street code and my family code were one and the same. So when anyone in my family failed, struggled, or needed my help, it was my unofficial sworn duty to do so. I put up bond money when they got locked away. I kept money on their books consistently, as if it were child support. When they came home, I gave when they asked and offered even when they didn't, sometimes when I barely had enough for myself. They were family, and I knew one day I could be in that same position. Our bond told me, "Help, they're all you got." But when it was my turn in the box, everything I had done was dismissed, looked at as nothing, forgotten, a misplaced memory. Their need to shine outshone my sacrifice. Behind my back, some ridiculed me; others left me for dead. Still, through it all, I kept the secrets we shared.

Somehow it became the opposite of the loyalty I assumed would never break. Outsiders were allowed to infiltrate us, especially when they were street affiliates. They were questioned less, and their presence somehow became more desired. I started to realize that I was replaceable. A new face could easily supersede an old one. New people bring new experiences, new hope, new fun, new ideas, and new opportunities, like a mother so consumed with a newborn that she forgets her first child. Whatever it was, it made it easier for some in my family to discard me for others or a quick dollar. Street money superseded old memories: a price tag on priceless memories came cheap.

Family and street life both had codes—and breaking either was one and the same. But I learned that family loyalty isn't guaranteed—it's a choice. And not everyone makes that choice. When bonds are broken, they're broken for a reason that is justifiable in someone else's mind, even if it feels like betrayal to you.

Phrases like "family comes first" and "blood is thicker than water" are drilled into us from an early age, shaping our understanding of loyalty and trust, while in the streets—and in life—family can be the most dangerous element, particularly when crime is involved. Unlike other affiliations, where membership is earned or vetted, family is automatic. It doesn't require a handshake, an agreement, or shared values—it's simply circumstance; you're born into it. This lack of criteria can make family bonds much more fragile, especially when tested by the harsh realities of street life.

In theory, family loyalty is supposed to be absolute. But in practice, I learned, it's more of a belief—a hope—that the people we share blood with will prioritize us. Street life has endlessly put that belief to the test, and history has shown that those tests at times fail. The consequences of misplaced trust in family can be devastating, particularly when survival is on the line. The truth is that self-interest frequently trumps loyalty, especially in families lacking a long tradition of support, unwavering commitment to one another, or a strong moral code to uphold the collective good.

Take the case of Carlton Brown, who received a 210-month federal prison sentence after his cousin turned informant against him in a drug trafficking case (*US v. Brown*, 8th Circuit, 1990). Carlton being family wasn't enough to prevent betrayal when the pressure of a federal investigation came down on his cousin and his cousin's family. This isn't an isolated incident. Stories like this are scattered throughout the pages of street history—stories of betrayal by people whose loyalty was assumed simply because they shared the same bloodline or family tree. Carlton Brown and many others found out that none of that matters.

The trials and tribulations surrounding this myth are countless. I've seen them play out in federal and state cases, as I spent time in these federal and state prisons watching fellow inmates being ratted out by family or deciding to rat on their own family. Testimonies and stories of betrayal serve as harsh reminders that family loyalty in street life is not as inherent as we'd like to believe. Loyalty requires a single, focused commitment, and it's impossible to divide that commitment between opposing parties. This creates a conflict for street affiliates. Who deserves their loyalty? Which code do they abide by—their family's or the streets'?

If someone's loyalty lies with the streets, their family or certain people in the family must tread carefully. The streets demand absolute loyalty, at least under the code, which often requires betraying family loyalty to maintain status or avoid consequences. Conversely, if someone prioritizes their family, it can be risky to trust them. They could easily rat to save their family or "do whatever it takes" to return home to them, maybe taking revenge during a street altercation, even if their family was in the wrong.

This loyalty dilemma, as I witnessed, often trapped individuals in a lose-lose situation. The streets demand sacrifices that family cannot bear, while family demands devotion that the streets won't tolerate. It's an impossible balance that often ends in betrayal, heartbreak, or destruction. It's an unnecessary tug-of-war, but fools like me did play the game.

Ultimately, the myth that family is always loyal persists because the thought is comforting. It gives us something to believe in when the world outside feels hostile. But comfort doesn't always equal truth, and pain doesn't always equal a lie. To put it simply, sometimes the truth hurts and a lie comforts.

In the streets, loyalty is rarely unconditional. Blood may bind us, but it doesn't seal us; it doesn't guarantee trust or allegiance. And when the stakes are high, family can be the first to falter, not because they're inherently bad, but because survival—how we want to spend or live the rest of our lives—often makes loyalty or relationships expendable.

True loyalty isn't dictated by blood. It's proven through actions, consistency, and sacrifice, and sometimes that's still not enough. And in the world of crime, where consequences are severe and temptations to betray are everywhere, loyalty is a scarce, fragile commodity. Recognizing this is not cynicism—it's intelligence, survival at its best.

> **THE TRUTH**
>
> A family is made of many parts. Each member's strength and loyalty are shaped by their character, beliefs, standards, desires, and upbringing. The true measure of those qualities isn't revealed until they're tested—often in ways no one expects. In the end, most people are loyal to themselves first, whether they're tied to blood or the streets. Selfishness is part of our nature, but the challenge is finding a collective goal that unites everyone. Without that shared purpose, without everyone moving in the same direction, holding to the same values, demanding accountability, "family" becomes just a word—stripped of its weight, stripped of its strength—and individuals are more strangers than family.

WHEN YOU ADD FAMILY TO THE STREET, LOYALTY BECOMES A DOUBLE BIND.

MYTH 12

THE HOOD IS YOUR FAMILY

> The hood offers unconditional love, protection, and support. No matter the ups and downs, the hood is family. It's hood love or no love. We ride together, and we die together.

"The hood is your family." This saying resonates deeply within urban environments, offering a comforting sense of belonging to anyone who yearns for connection. It presents the hood as more than just a geographical location on a map—the hood becomes a lifeline, a source of identity, and for some, a surrogate family. For many, it's the only constant in a world of instability, offering a name they can speak aloud and know they'll be met with love, honor, respect, and perhaps even fear.

For decades, the hood has been a place of hardship and survival. The goal for many is simply to make it to the next day. For others, it's about finding purpose in something greater than themselves, delaying their worries for the future. Bonds form quickly in such environments—many out of necessity, many others through leisure. Loyalty becomes the currency of relationships, and collective identities can feel stronger than biological ties. For those who grew up without the love and guidance of parents or guardians, these connections often fill the role of the family they never had.

At times, these bonds come with a great cost as substance abuse becomes fashionable and normalized. Because of this, the relationships forged in the hood can turn into cycles of codependency. What began as camaraderie spirals into chaos and violence, transforming friendships into rivalries and alliances into opposing factions. The very relationships that are meant to be supportive become destructive, leaving many trapped in whirlwinds of dysfunction that they cannot easily escape.

The term *the hood* was popularized—and perhaps even coined—in the early 1980s by predominantly Black and Brown youth in inner cities as shorthand for "the neighborhood." When rap music, primarily gangster rap, began to rise, songs like "Boyz-n-the Hood" by Eazy-E, released in 1997 and followed by a movie of the same name in 1991, cemented and glamorized the term. Soon it was a common phrase, becoming synonymous with terms like *the bricks, the turf, the block, the ave,* and most famously *the set,* as many would ask, "What set you from?" reflecting a growing culture of territoriality and gang life.

As rap music began to glorify the struggles and pride of ghetto life, *the hood* replaced the word *community* in popular discourse, often with a negative connotation—being spoken with aggression, force, and even a deadly outcome depending on when it was said and whom it was said to. The hood became both a badge of honor and a trap—a contradiction in itself—something to represent, but also something to escape. Some found themselves so attached to the hood that they were unwilling to venture outside of it.

The neighborhood, at its core and by definition, is simply a geographic location—a cluster of homes situated within a certain proximity to one another. A community, however, is something deeper: the emotional and social fabric that binds people together with a sense of purpose. A true community uplifts, supports, guides, and prepares its members to engage meaningfully with the broader world. But when communities turn on themselves—when they fight, "beef," go to war, and kill one another—those communal bonds collapse. What remains is not a community, but the fractured aftermath of a war zone, where the idea of family becomes distant and the hope for unity is nearly extinct.

In this fractured space, the glorification of the hood masked deeper failures. Stanley "Tookie" Williams, co-founder of the Crips, exposed this illusion in his book *Blue Rage, Black Redemption*, reflecting on how growing up in South Central meant being fed a steady diet of hopelessness—where poverty, violence, and negative stereotypes worked together to lock young Black minds into cycles of inferiority and self-destruction. He described how he internalized the myth that Black people were inherently criminal, uneducated, and undeserving—left to claw for crumbs of the so-called American Dream, which claimed to reward effort but rarely delivered rewards equally.

This toxic narrative caused many children to be neglected by their own parents and constantly overlooked by systems designed to protect them; generations of children were plainly forgotten. Even policies like the No Child Left Behind Act of 2001—intended to provide educational equity—failed to reach many in these communities. The hood stepped in and embraced many of those left behind, in most cases offering a false sense of refuge while conditioning their minds to accept limited horizons. It blinded many to possibilities beyond its borders: higher education, spiritual growth, political participation, and the constructive experiences needed to build thriving communities.

Still, the myth that "the hood is your family" endured, promising that you would never stand alone, cementing itself in the language of belonging, framed as family, using kindred terms like *cuzz* for cousins, *folks* for family, *blood* for bonds, and *brother* for kinship. But beneath these endearing labels lies a harsh reality: deception, selfishness, and manipulation often masquerade as loyalty. The hood perpetuates an illusion of equality and solidarity, but this facade quickly dissolves under the pressures of greed and survival. Lines blur between love and hate, respect and jealousy, family and foes. In the end, it can easily become every person for themselves.

For some, the hood is all they have—no mother or father, no grandparents, no family to love or sacrifice for them. Their only viable source is street life, which demands an outrageous price. In the hood, some children grow up with forced adult obligations, scrambling for their needs and not their wants, and are shaped by circumstances beyond their control. The cycle of victimhood becomes a different kind of hood—one that leaves the deepest mental and emotional scars. Escaping it is nearly impossible without significant support, as survival alone demands more than most can carry.

Over time, the term *the hood* spread beyond lower-class communities, becoming part of the vernacular among the lower middle class, the middle class, and even beyond. As gang life and street culture gained prominence, the myth that "the hood is your family" began to ensnare a broader generation, leaving many lost, forgotten, or killed off. The hood's promise of community gave way to a culture of individualism where betrayal, violence, and survival by any means replaced neighborly support and generational togetherness. No one wanted to borrow sugar anymore; they just took it. Everything became a competition. Drug sales, substance abuse, and greed became normalized, as the pursuit of money overshadowed the need for unity. What had once been a community disintegrated into a collection of isolated individuals, each looking out for themselves. Cornel West once reflected that while 1967 wasn't a perfect time, there was a stronger sense of community back then than in 1997—a reminder that even in difficult eras, the bonds between people were often more intact than in later decades.

The myth that "the hood is your family" offers a seductive promise of belonging, but it can easily be a double-edged sword. While it provides identity and connection, it also ensnares its members in a web of limited opportunity, false loyalty, and destructive cycles. It offers love, but in many cases it demands a price—a price too heavy for most to bear.

STREET VIEW

I was transient throughout my childhood, moving from place to place, city to city, to many different gang-infested neighborhoods. On average, I would move at least once every year. That kind of life took a toll on me; it was destabilizing, especially when compounded with the many other challenges I faced. Yet it also gave me the chance to see that these neighborhoods had more commonalities than differences.

I quickly learned, growing up in these hoods, that it was in my best interest to avoid mistakes at all costs, especially when adapting to street life—there was no place for trial and error. The comforting idea of "I'll get it right next time" could be a deadly delusion, even for a child. To find solace in all this, I started believing the myth that "the hood is your family." For a lonely kid like me, those words offered comfort and togetherness, healing and growth. I thought the raw passion I felt from people in these neighborhoods reflected my own loneliness, abandonment issues, emotional pain, and yearning for my basic needs to be met. In all, I was confused and looking for guidance without contradictions, and I was willing to be that family member of the hood who would sacrifice it all.

But as I would come to learn, the hood was not a family. It was a harsh ecosystem filled with struggles that varied from home to home or person to person. While some kids struggled and even cried themselves to sleep because their basic needs—like food, clothing, and proper living conditions—weren't being met, others were experiencing the beauty of having one or more loving and responsible parents or grandparents to guide them and offer them more than they were seeing. But for many of them, for some reason, that still wasn't enough.

I remember a homie in one particular neighborhood whose mother worked tirelessly to give him everything he wanted and needed. Unlike some of us, he had the basics and more—name-brand clothes, the latest tech, even opportunities to travel. But at fifteen, when his mother told him it was time to get a summer job so he could start to contribute to his own wants and needs, he turned to dealing drugs, claiming no one was there for him but the streets. Needless to say, he, like many of us, wound up in prison. Another buddy of mine had a father who was considered "strict" and wanted to instill a work ethic in him. Instead of appreciating this guidance and embracing his father's wisdom, he played the victim to his mother and grandmother, who worked against his father and let him move in with his grandmother. Gaining the freedom he wanted, he joined a gang in her neighborhood, became one of their main "shooters," and wound up getting a life sentence.

These situations aren't unique; they are relatable in some

way or another to many different situations in many hoods. No matter the circumstances, the outcomes are usually harsh and often cause regret and confusion.

By the time I started seriously questioning these things, I myself had created a habit—living a lifestyle that I had no clue how to stop—and was spiraling out of control.

The hood, if anything, is surely complex. But if it were a family, it would be a dysfunctional one, made up of drug dealers, false leaders, dope spots, liquor stores, religious hypocrites, crooked cops, killers, wannabes, snitches, hustlers, backstabbers, alcoholics, dope fiends, sideline cheerleaders, daydreamers—and of course, gangsters. Together, these individuals and many others outside the hood create a chaotic ecosystem, each playing their part in its existence and its dysfunction.

Once upon a time, many of these hoods were known as communities but were ravaged by these individuals and outside political forces alike. While the definition of the term *community* was never degraded, over time, a connotation of *the hood* was elevated, which led to the glorification of the poverty and dysfunction we all woke up to every day. Some people managed to escape and never returned, while others came back with their success and wealth and agitated, glorified, elevated, and encouraged the same dysfunction they claimed to despise. Some returned without any level of fame or big bank accounts but still worked energetically in the hopes of making a difference—giving a new generation an opportunity to see the world or simply their own environments as something greater than they were being portrayed as. Although many who live in these neighborhoods and many who do not work tirelessly at making a difference, there are so many others who prefer the status quo. It's a tug-of-war over whether every neighborhood can become a community again.

The hood, once a symbol of survival, became a brand that outsiders wore, imitated, and flaunted without paying the same price as those who lived it or lived in it every day. Corporate America and entertainers from many genres turned the hood's culture, image, stories, and raw energy into profit. While many bragged about their connections to the hood, speaking its language and reflecting or imitating its style, few actually wanted to live there. They took what they could but rarely, if ever, gave anything back—illustrating one more difference between a hood and a community.

> **THE TRUTH**
>
> Family moves in unity, like a community bound by loyalty, rules, and, most of all, an unwavering shared purpose. When that accord is broken, the unit ceases to be a family and becomes a philosophy of survival: every man, woman, and child for themselves—individualism. Even when connected by blood, the concept of family becomes no more than a name, a hollow label that holds no meaning when this accord is broken. The hood is built on many characters and personalities that can love you and hate you at the same time. It can offer you guidance and destruction simultaneously. The hood is not a family of unity; it's a boot camp to test your abilities for street life and life in general.

IF THE HOOD IS A FAMILY, IT'S DYSFUNCTIONAL.

MYTH 13

GANGSTERS AIN'T GAY

> The essence of manhood is rooted in strength—both physical and spiritual. To be dominated by another man, whether emotionally, physically, or sexually, is a betrayal of that strength, a symbol of weakness and servitude. Power is the ultimate measure of masculinity, and the streets demand unwavering power. Gangsters are strong, and homosexuality is weak, and anybody who disagrees is spiritually bankrupt and sure as fuck ain't no gangster.

Street life has long perpetuated the belief that certain actions or identities are incompatible with being a gangster. Among these is the myth that gangsters should not or cannot be gay—a notion deeply entrenched in the culture's rigid ideals of masculinity. For decades, in street life, it was said that there were four things a man could never recover from: snitching, child molestation, rape, and homosexuality. This belief allowed the myth of the heterosexual gangster to flourish, creating an environment where any discussion of homosexuality is met with denial, ridicule, or outright violence.

Historical examples reveal the consequences of this myth. In 1992, John "Johnny Boy" D'Amato, head of the DeCavalcante family in New Jersey, was murdered after rumors surfaced about his relationships with men. Similarly, Robert Mormando, a hitman for the crime family La Cosa Nostra, lived secretly as a gay man until he revealed his truth in court while cooperating with authorities. Despite such revelations, the myth endures, and homosexuality is treated as a betrayal of the "macho" gangster image.

The rejection of homosexuality in street life parallels societal prejudices and the many institutions—religious, political, or cultural—that have historically denounced it.

Within the criminal underworld, these attitudes are compounded by a fear that accepting homosexuality will tarnish the hypermasculine image of gangsterism—an image long associated with dominance, aggression, and heterosexual prowess. If you defy these norms, you will often face severe consequences: ostracism, violence, or even death. In hip-hop culture—especially within gangster rap—many prominent voices, such as Snoop Dogg, BG Knocc Out, DaBaby, DMX, and Boosie Badazz, have openly spoken out against LGBTQ+ communities, reinforcing these rigid gender and sexual expectations. In recent years, however, some have attempted to walk back their past remarks, citing growth and acknowledging that hip-hop culture or culture in general should evolve to reflect the full spectrum of life, including street life. Yet as author Ernest Gaines once challenged, it's telling that society is often more comfortable seeing two men hold guns than hold hands—a sobering reflection of the values we choose to normalize and those we continue to reject.

Still, in a life of crime, there's a glaring double standard that continues to exist. Women in street life are rarely subjected to the same scrutiny as men. Female homosexuality is often accepted, even celebrated. Women can adopt what is commonly known as "masculine" traits, form relationships with other women, and still remain embraced by their peers. Rappers like Young M.A illustrate this vividly—in her breakout hit "OOOUUU," she brags about taking an older woman home from the club while hoping to bring along the woman's daughter, a flex met not with judgment, but with nods of approval. She isn't the only one—artists such as Yung Miami (of City Girls) have also woven open references to bisexuality into their music and public persona without damaging their street credibility. This disparity reflects broader cultural attitudes that hypersexualize female homosexuality while criminalizing or stigmatizing male homosexuality.

Street life, much like society at large, is not governed by a universal set of rules or beliefs. Each group, gang, or region operates with its own "personal politics," and what is taboo in one circle may be overlooked in another. While gangsters often share a disdain for outside authority, their personal views on moral issues, including sexuality, vary widely.

Even institutions as notoriously hypermasculine and homophobic as the Mafia have had to shift. In 2019, PinkNews reported on a significant change: the Italian Mafia dropped its total ban on homosexuality after discovering that the son of a prominent mob boss was a drag queen. This revelation forced the organization to confront its own prejudices and adapt to the changing social landscape.

The larger, more diverse, and less secretive street life becomes, the more diluted its original, hardcore philosophies become. New members bring new ideas and challenges to traditional norms, often reshaping the culture over time. Even religious influences, which have historically framed homosexuality as a sin, may fade in significance as generational shifts occur. While some gangsters view rejecting homosexuality as a way to remain "holy" in their religious beliefs despite a life of treachery and crime, these contradictions highlight the complex and often hypocritical nature of street morality. As some have observed, we all carry contradictions within us—the saint and the criminal, the refined and the reckless. Instead of trying to eliminate one side, we learn to live with both.

Ultimately, the myth that "gangsters ain't gay" persists because it upholds outdated notions of masculinity and power. Yet as society progresses and individuals continue to defy stereotypes, the cracks in this myth become increasingly visible.

STREET VIEW

Ever since I was a child, the word *gangster* has carried weight. It wasn't just a label—it was a persona, and never one associated with softness or vulnerability. The word came packaged with rebellion, bravery, cold humor, sharp style, and a presumedly hardened spirit shaped by survival. Behind the allure were brutal stories—tales of violence, loss, and constant struggle. There was nothing gentle about it, no matter how cool it may have seemed.

Gangsterism was built on rawness and unfiltered reality. It was a lifestyle steeped in masculinity, dominance, and a tough exterior. Gangsters were often seen as womanizers, usually surrounded by beautiful women who seemed to be drawn to them regardless of how they were treated. These men and their lives were associated with coming from poverty, with little formal education, yet they still carried power and status—especially with women.

According to the dictionary, a gangster is simply someone in a gang who engages in violent or criminal acts. It was never a gender-exclusive title. I knew plenty of female gangbangers—many of them just as tough as the men, and in some cases even tougher. Some retained their femininity, while others adopted a more rugged, masculine style—driving lowriders or other "muscle cars," carrying themselves with confidence, gripping gun handles, and having romantic relationships that mirrored those of their male counterparts. In fact, Queen Latifah's character in *Set It Off* (1996) was not a fictional stretch but a reflection of what many of us had already seen in real life, long before Hollywood gave the character a name or a face.

Everyone had their own image of a gangster—an old Italian man in a suit, a young Black man in streetwear with his pants below his butt, a Latino in oversized pants that seemed to be pulled up to his chest, or even a short Asian man who spoke softly and kept his face emotionless. They all wore black shades, typically Locs.

These images shaped cultural assumptions and led to powerful myths, one of them being that a true gangster couldn't possibly be gay. Why? Because in many of these circles, gangsterism was woven tightly into a warped definition of manhood—one where emotions were weaknesses and masculinity was equated with control, aggression, and heterosexual dominance.

Even the "working man," who took pride in legal labor, would define manhood by hard work and responsibility, while a gangster might argue that abiding by society's laws and subjecting oneself to struggling unnecessarily in a financial way made one less of a man or not a man at all. The one thing both often agreed on was this: no real man was gay. And that's where the myth began—and still stubbornly survives.

While outsiders in our environments adopted whatever image they saw as gangster, gangsters shaped their own internal code, including beliefs, expectations of each other, and rules—some written, most unwritten, but all enforced without compromise. The most aggressively upheld street codes that I can recall, across the spectrum of gangsters, were:

"No snitches. No rapists. No faggots."

These were the three cardinal sins of the streets. You could even be a coward, and sometimes, some individuals would allow you to redeem yourself. But these? If you broke any of these three, you were done with.

That was the creed, as far back as I can remember. No matter your race, religion, or background, if you were in the streets, this was law. That's why gay gangsters never exposed themselves. In a world where being "real" is everything, ironically, being honest about who you are could get you killed.

For many years—and even now—the image of homosexuality stains what many consider "authentic" street life, no matter how cool some gangster rappers try to make a man wearing a dress or painting his nails seem.

I grew up in the inner cities at a time when those things were not tolerated; they were shunned, and the word *faggot* was flung around like dead leaves in a tornado. When children are raised in an environment full of defiance, crime, and confusion, topped with older gangsters condemning homosexuality, their hate and their actions toward homosexuals are only intensified.

Even mothers who deeply loved their children sometimes needed time alone for prayer or silence to accept a child being gay. Fathers, on the other hand, were often more brutal and resistant, especially with their sons. Still, while all of this played out in homes and in hearts, gangs and homosexuality rose side by side in our communities. That rise made it inevitable that the two would in some way intertwine: gay gangsters would eventually be exposed.

I met many throughout my time in the streets. Three died of AIDS, a tragedy in itself. But just being associated with a gay man, whether you knew he was gay or not, could make your reputation suspect. And in a world that was already dangerous, hanging out openly with homosexual men, even out of friendliness, could easily "put a jacket" on you. only adding more heat to your already heated everyday world. If you continued after being warned, you would hear, "You *really* askin' for it."

And yet, for many gay gangsters, homosexuality became a profitable hustle.

The gangster image holds power—it fascinates many, especially men outside the street world. Gay outsiders have been known to pay "top dollar" for what they call bad boys or, to put it bluntly, gangster dick.

Some gangsters get propositioned for a "one-time thing," and for those who accept, it quickly becomes a job, a side hustle, a secret life. The money, luxury cars, designer clothes, jewelry, cosignings, and business support that they can receive start to boost their game—and their image. They justify it by saying, "As long as I'm not getting fucked..." But soon everything becomes fair game. They become everything they said they wouldn't be. They dive headfirst into the world they once condemned—for what Sheila E. called "The Glamorous Life."

I started to see street life—the code and the identity—exposed by vanity, greed, curiosity, or biological needs. The place I once took pride in was not invaded by homosexuality; it had always been there, lying dormant. Eventually, change had to come.

But as the myth "gangsters ain't gay" shaped our understanding of others, it also shaped how we saw ourselves. We inherited a street code that was full of contradictions. It demanded strength but allowed the strong to abuse the weak. It condemned homosexuality but, in many cases, turned a blind eye to the rape of men in prison. Falling in love with another man was seen as wrong, but dominating him sexually—in the name of power—was somehow, in the eyes of some gangsters, not gay.

As a child, I heard the stories—horrific, whispered tales of boys raped in juvenile halls by other boys, and men being conquered in prisons. These weren't just stories. They were warnings, cautionary tales. If you chose the streets, you would be choosing the possibility of prison. And in prison, your manhood might be put to the test in more ways than one.

But no one talked about the twisted logic behind it all. No one questioned how a man could rape another man and still claim to be a gangster without irony.

In due time, I was incarcerated myself, and there, I saw the hypocrisy up close. Many who condemned homosexuality on the streets were later exposed for engaging in it behind bars. Gayness in prison transcended race and religion. It didn't care what gang you claimed or what religion you followed as long as you were down for the "nitty gritty."

I saw men who, at some point, transformed themselves to look like women, and some were quite convincing—creating what I called an optical illusion, an attempt to blur the lines between femininity and masculinity in places already charged with power and desire.

Just by existing as visibly queer, some of these individuals automatically created tension. Their presence alone could escalate violence as men would see the optical illusion as a personal possession. In a place like prison, where control and respect meant everything, homosexuality didn't just challenge the rules; it exposed how fragile those rules really were. It forced people to confront what they refused to admit: that the street code had cracks, and those cracks were widening over time.

Still, being openly gay in prison wasn't just dangerous—it

could be deadly. There was an unofficial but widely understood law: "Be discreet or get yo ass beat." That meant you didn't parade your sexuality, you didn't show affection publicly, and you didn't draw attention to what you did behind closed doors because many gangsters in prison still held up this cardinal rule. Some yards might tolerate it. Others wouldn't. Depending on where you landed, being known as a gay gangster could get you ostracized or worse.

Even your association with someone known to be gay could bring you your own troubles, just as it did on the streets. Guilt by association was real. What you thought of as innocent interactions could easily be seen by others as overindulgence or unacceptable. And once suspicion was cast on you, it didn't matter whether it was true or not. The damage could already be done. So the best solution was to eliminate yourself from the problem once you were told of it.

Some men explained their homosexual behavior with disclaimers like "I only do it in prison; it helps me pass the time"—as if setting boundaries around space and circumstances made it less real or unofficial. But the truth didn't need to explain itself. It just existed. And it existed everywhere.

The myth that "gangstas ain't gay" was never about fact. It was about fear: fear of softness, fear of vulnerability, fear of being seen as weak. Add to that the weight of religion, cultural pride, and generational ignorance, and the myth became a kind of armor that we wore to protect ourselves from uncomfortable truths.

Yet behind those walls, away from the streets and the image people fought to maintain, something else became clear: sexuality is more fluid than most are willing to admit. And gangsterism is not exempt from contradiction, shame, or desire.

Prison doesn't just test your strength. It tests everything—your principles, your beliefs, your desires, your identity. The person you thought you were might get shaken to the core. Many men inside say, "Prison don't create faggots—that shit was already in you before you got here." I didn't argue for or against that belief; I saw it as just another possibility stacked on many. But still, it reinforces the fact that there are gangsters on the streets who are gay, carrying a secret beyond their crimes.

What's certain is this: there are gangsters who are gay—some out and open, some hiding in silence, some balancing both worlds. Whether the streets want to accept them or not, they exist. That alone is enough to bust the myth. The myth doesn't hold because the reality is louder.

In street life, secrets are currency. And sometimes the biggest secret isn't about the crimes you've committed, but the identity you've hidden just to survive.

THE TRUTH

Sexuality exists independently of the roles or identities people assume, including being a gangster. Street life is about survival, power, and reputation, but none of these inherently dictate a person's sexual orientation. The myth stems from rigid perceptions of masculinity and the fear of vulnerability in environments where strength is prized. However, gangsters, like anyone else, come from diverse backgrounds and have equally diverse and independent identities. Denying this reality only reinforces harmful stereotypes and limits the understanding of human complexity within street culture.

GANGSTERS ARE DIVERSE.

MYTH 14

STREET DUDES DON'T CRY

> Crying is for the weak; it is an intolerable act for the strong. It is shameful and embarrassing, and will receive no favors. In the streets, only the strong will survive, and the tears of a man expose his inner child, which could be a liability. Real men tough it out because they will be taken advantage of if they don't.

"Street dudes don't cry," or more commonly "gangsters don't cry," is a myth deeply rooted in the expectation of toughness—a belief that to survive in the streets, one must show no vulnerability, no weakness, and certainly no tears. Emotions such as fear, pain, frustration, and even joy are often suppressed, as their display is seen as compromising one's strength and reliability. Phrases like "be a man," "real men don't cry," "stop acting like a bitch," or "ain't shit funny" are not just insults but directives designed to enforce an image of stoicism, particularly among street affiliates.

In street culture, crying is equated with breaking under pressure. Whether facing the threat of incarceration, physical assault, or heartbreak, shedding tears is seen as a failure to maintain control. Instigators in the streets—both male and female—often exploit emotional displays, treating them as weaknesses to be weaponized. In other contexts, this might be labeled "bullying," but in the streets, it is normalized and sometimes even celebrated as a way to be seen as separating the "strong" from the "weak." This relentless pressure keeps many street affiliates on edge, constantly "on their toes," unable to relax or show true emotions for fear of being "caught slipping" or reimagined—being seen differently. Even Seth Green—who isn't from the streets—once pointed out the strange mix of emotions involved in watching someone break down: it can hit you as both heartbreaking and oddly funny at the same time. That irony reflects how desensitized many people are to pain, especially in environments where vulnerability is entertainment, not empathy, so many will suppress those emotions.

Ironically, this suppression of emotion is often misinterpreted as strength. Yet research—found in Medical News Today—shows that crying has numerous physical and emotional benefits. It soothes the body, relieves stress, enhances mood, aids sleep, and even improves vision. It also provides an outlet for emotional release, a way to process the burdens of life. By denying themselves this outlet, many internalize their struggles, creating an emotional dam that builds over time.

This internalization is particularly dangerous because it often leads to depression, a condition that is pervasive but largely undiagnosed in street life. Many individuals who are drawn to crime also abuse substances as an escape from emotional pain, but the harsh realities of street life only compound those struggles. Without access to resources, family support, or proper guidance, depression festers, masked by the very stoicism street affiliates are taught to uphold.

Even legendary musician Ray Charles once confessed that he had done his share of crying, especially when there was no other way to contain his feelings. He recognized that crying is feeling, and feeling is being human. Ray wasn't from the streets, but his words cut to the core of a truth many street dudes aren't willing to say out loud—suppressing emotions doesn't necessarily make you strong. If done too often, it can slowly break you and create confusion in how you feel about yourself and others.

For children involved in street life, the damage is even more profound. Suppressing emotions from a young age can carry into adulthood, creating patterns of unaddressed trauma and mental health issues. The fear of being seen as weak or vulnerable prevents many from seeking help, especially when societal institutions are perceived as hostile or contemptuous. For many in the streets, their distrust of authority is not unfounded; it is rooted in experiences of mistreatment and systemic neglect. The older an individual gets, the thicker the layers become that insulate that child who never received the proper interactions they needed. As writer Tamara Kulish has pointed out, the message that "boys don't cry" becomes a lifelong burden, making it hard for men to fully process or express their emotions.

Ultimately, in the streets, that burden becomes even heavier, as the myth that "street dudes don't cry" or even that street dudes shouldn't cry is both a coping mechanism and a trap. While it offers some facade of strength, it denies those individuals—male and female—the healing and growth that come from confronting their emotions openly. In a world as unforgiving as the streets, the refusal to cry might seem like survival, but in reality, it can become a slow, silent erosion of the self.

STREET VIEW

Street life is a relentless cycle of chaos, pain, and survival, yet in all the mayhem, I rarely saw street affiliates cry. For all the suffering, loss, and grief we encountered, the lack of tears was striking, but as many would say, they were just smiling to keep from crying. However, that's not to say I never saw street dudes cry—I did. Some broke down, their emotions spilling out like a dam bursting. I wasn't surprised to see certain individuals crying. But when I saw the "hardcore gangsters," the men I thought were unshakable, breaking into sobs, it left me rattled. These moments were unexpected lessons, forcing me to confront my deeply ingrained beliefs about manhood, vulnerability, and the complexity of human emotions—all that mixed with gangsterism.

From as far back as I can remember, I wasn't comfortable with emotions, especially painful ones. Tears, particularly from men who carried the weight of the streets, unsettled me. They didn't evoke my empathy as much as they left me distant, unsure of how to engage with someone so visibly vulnerable. Like many others, I grew up equating tears with weakness or unpreparedness, believing they were an unacceptable response to the realities of life. My mindset wasn't just shaped by what I saw but also by what I experienced throughout my life—in and out of the streets.

I remember the last time I cried—I was about seventeen years old. My mother, with a calm and cutting voice, told me I was an embarrassment to her because I was the last of her children and had followed in the footsteps of my older brother and sisters and become a street affiliate. Because of that, she wished she had aborted me when she first contemplated it. She told me that the only reason I was alive was because she'd missed her appointment to do so. I cried that day—not just cried, but sobbed uncontrollably because her words were like a blade, carving out parts of my soul that I didn't know could hurt. I was still a child—once a momma's boy—my hardships and battles hadn't fully stripped that away. But this pain was like no other, one I had to face and make sense of entirely on my own.

I'd faced the streets head-on by then—being shot at, jumped, robbed, and assaulted in unspeakable ways by police officers, losing friends who were killed, and being openly hated by family. Some of those moments tore me to pieces, but my mother's words shattered me in ways that an attempt on my life or police brutality could never. I realized in that moment that tears weren't only a sign of failure or fragility. They were evidence of pain too deep to suppress, a necessary release for survival.

Looking back, I now understand those tears at seventeen. They weren't a sign of defeat—they were my body's way of recalibrating after an emotional blow. They prepared me for the harsh truths of life—truths that I could only learn through experience and that would continue to test me. They reminded me that pain isn't always avoidable; in fact, it's often the cost of connection, hope, love, or loyalty. It's nothing to be ashamed of, just something to be mindful of. And over time, I felt the sting of many other losses, including the quiet distance from people I once stood close to and those I adored. There may not have been tears in those moments, but it hurt almost the same.

The streets and some households across the country teach us to suppress emotions, to be stone-faced and impenetrable—to fail to achieve emotional maturity. But this myth that street dudes don't cry is dangerous. It makes us ashamed of one of the most human ways of processing any type of pain. Crying doesn't necessarily mean you're weak; it means you're alive. Every tear tells a story, marking a pivotal moment in your life—a comma in your sentence, an exclamation mark in your paragraph, or the end of a chapter before another begins.

Street dudes cry—maybe not often, maybe not publicly—but there are many who do, more than you can probably imagine. And the tears of a clown can only hide for so long. Suppressing tears doesn't make pain disappear. If anything, it has the potential to amplify pain, creating fractures in the spirit that manifest in destructive ways. I've come to learn that tears can be a source of strength, helping us regain balance and perspective. Vulnerability isn't necessarily weakness—at times it's growth, even when it feels like breaking.

During my time in various court-mandated programs, ranging from AA (Alcoholics Anonymous) to NA (Narcotics Anonymous) and RDAP (the Residential Drug Abuse Program, a therapeutic initiative), I witnessed many gangsters cry. And let me be clear: their tears didn't make them any less menacing. These were still the same dudes who would beat the brakes off you if you tested their gangster. But those moments of vulnerability weren't about weakness. They were about release, about confronting the parts of their lives they had either buried deep or forgotten altogether. Some of those issues were unresolved; others never had a chance to surface until that moment. But in facing those hidden wounds, they weren't just reflecting on pain; they were rediscovering the paths that led them there in the first place. Crying became a doorway, not a defeat. It was a step toward understanding who they were, how they got there, and maybe—just maybe—who they could still become.

In a world where suffering is abundant and emotional armor is a survival tool, crying is still a deeply human act. It connects us to ourselves, reminds us of our humanity, and, in its own way, teaches us how to move forward. Crying doesn't diminish your strength as a man or a street affiliate; it reinforces it. After all, even the toughest exteriors can't contain the weight of the world, as we are nothing more than a tiny fraction of it.

THE TRUTH

Tears are the oceans inside our souls, and they are strong enough to break down the walls and the barriers we have built within us. Like water overtopping a structure, weakening concrete, or breaking through a levee, tears have a tendency to wash away all the built-up pain, as street life can build a lot within us. Tears can help us gradually knock down old structures, reconstruct something new, and make us stronger, if we allow it.

TEARS FROM THE STREETS ARE REDEMPTIVE.

MYTH 15

PEOPLE WHO LOOK STREET WILL BE STREET

> The streets don't allow fakers and pretenders, posers and wannabes; they're filled with real motherfuckers, and they don't sugarcoat shit. You either real or you ain't—simple as that. What you see is what you get; there are no filters in street life. The streets are too dangerous and raw to let someone fake their way through.

The streets condition many, if not most, to believe that if someone looks the part, they are the part: dangerous, ruthless, unafraid to pull the trigger. They are seen as soldiers in the trenches, solidified, "street."

Even police officers buy into this myth. It's called profiling. So in the world of street life, where perception shapes reality, looking like a gangster becomes a prophecy. If you wear the costume or talk with the vernacular, many believe you've earned it—and therein lies the myth. But the truth? It becomes far more complicated as reality is fused with illusions and stereotypes.

When cultures are obsessed with appearances, it's easy to fall into the trap of equating someone's look with their lifestyle. Pop culture, street culture, and society at large thrive on stereotypes, reducing individuals to their attire, mannerisms, and attitudes. For those associated with street life, this perception becomes even more entrenched. Tattoos, slang, certain attire, and a defiant swagger often serve as the uniform of "street credibility," but reality is far more nuanced. Looking the part doesn't guarantee someone is living, dying, or willing to kill for the part.

Those in street life may challenge the myth by boldly saying, "This ain't a myth—real ones can spot the fake ones from a mile away." But then there's the contradiction when they say, "There are so many real ones dead or in jail behind these fake muthafuckas."

Even the sharpest minds, the most seasoned vets in the game of street life, get fooled. That's because talking the part, wearing the costume, and playing the role is a skill in itself—one that some learn better than others. Looks and appearances are like magic tricks—they dazzle the eye and distract the mind. They entertain, seduce, and offer hope to those looking for "partners in crime." This is why law enforcement is among the greatest illusionists of all time. They dress and appear to be a part of the streets, giving street affiliates what they are looking for—a worm on a hook or crankbait. If someone fits your expectations, they become much easier for you to trust and more likable. And when trust is currency, appearance can be a counterfeit bill.

"Illusion is the first of all pleasures."

—VOLTAIRE

Joaquin Garcia was an FBI agent who infiltrated the Mafia for twenty-four years as a self-proclaimed jewel thief under the name of "Jack Falcone." Joseph Pistone, famously known as Donnie Brasco, spent six years inside the Mafia, undetected. These men didn't just blend in—they became trusted, embraced, and protected.

For street dudes, being fooled by someone in uniform is often more painful, more humiliating, and sometimes more costly than being crossed by one of their own, as they may have to spend a substantial amount of time behind bars, thinking about how they failed to recognize a real agent of the law "playing street."

Street life attracts the common person for a variety of reasons—necessity, survival, or allure—and if you merely "look or sound the part" without living it, you are often dismissed as a "poseur," "wannabe," or "perpetrator," adopting the aesthetic of street life without engaging in its risks or responsibilities. These individuals never fully grasp the dangers ahead as they try to have one foot in and one foot out. When they enter this world, they don't consider the collateral damage: family members targeted by rivals, betrayal by peers, or the physical toll of violence and imprisonment. These are consequences that no appearance can prepare someone for.

Interestingly, most people who enter street life do so between the ages of eleven and fifteen, a developmental stage where decision-making is dominated by impulsivity. And studies highlight that the brain's frontal lobe—the region responsible for rational thought and long-term planning—doesn't fully mature until about age twenty-five. This underdevelopment of the brain, compounded by substance abuse, impairs the brain further, affecting judgment and self-control well into adulthood.

This may suggest that most individuals in street life participate out of habit. Regardless of the narrative, this formative period shapes not only their identity but also society's perception of them, which creates a thin line between appearance and reality.

Meanwhile, some criminals defy street stereotypes altogether, blending in seamlessly with society, presenting themselves as upstanding, respectable citizens while secretly living double lives. These individuals avoid the spotlight, shun street theatrics, and quietly hope to never be discovered. Take Barney Harris, for example. He was a high school basketball coach and mentor who appeared to be dedicated to shaping young athletes' futures. To those around him, he was a role model, a man of discipline and integrity. But behind that polished exterior, Harris was deeply entrenched in the drug trade. His hidden life came crashing down when he attempted to rob a Mexican cartel, a decision that ended in a deadly shootout and ultimately exposed the dangerous world he had been operating in all along.

Harris is far from the only one. There are countless others—men and women who show up as model citizens by day but live criminal lives behind closed doors. They dress the part, speak the language of legal-social success, and walk confidently through mainstream society while quietly orchestrating illegal operations—blue-collar and white-collar crimes. Ironically, many of these individuals live the life that some in the streets only pretend to. Their ability to mask their true nature is often refined, calculated, and difficult to detect with the naked eye.

This unsettling truth can be found in state and federal prisons, where those who once held prestigious careers as federal judges, law enforcement officers, doctors, entertainers, CEOs, attorneys, and real estate developers are now stripped of their titles and doing time for serious crimes, including drug trafficking, fraud, human trafficking, murder, murder for hire, and even organized crime conspiracies. Their presence behind bars challenges every visual cue we've been taught to associate with criminality. It reveals that crime isn't always loud, flashy, or dressed in sagging pants and accompanied by street slang.

Street life has also become an open performance. Social media, music, and entertainment have commercialized their images, turning them into bigger spectacles. What was once said to be a closed, insular world has now been woven into mainstream culture, accepted as the norm in many places and is open to anyone who can play the role of a gangster. These "gang-stars" are chameleons, skilled at mimicking the gangsters they've seen in movies or documentaries. Street life is torn between reality and a show in which drugs and alcohol help many give their best performance.

The myth that "people who look street will be street" persists because it simplifies a complex reality. But appearances can be deceiving. True street life isn't defined by clothing or demeanor; it's defined by choices, circumstances, and consequences that everyone must deal with when they arise—none of which are visible at first glance.

STREET VIEW

I grew up in a time when pretending was second nature. Having imaginary friends, playing war or cowboys and "Indians", and building forts—it was all as normal as riding bikes, shooting marbles, or walking to the store with a handwritten note to buy cigarettes for our parents. But the games we played weren't just made up out of nowhere. They were heavily shaped by the world around us—TV shows, movies, music, and the people in our communities. We mimicked what we saw, and we believed it.

One of our favorite games was cops and robbers. Strangely enough, unlike most of the kids, I wanted to be the cop. In my young eyes, cops were heroes—protectors of the weak, defenders of the innocent, and symbols of law and order. I loved the idea of the badge and uniform. I'd shape my fingers into a gun and yell, "Freeze!"—fully convinced I was standing on the side of justice. But my admiration didn't last long.

It all began to change the moment I saw those same "heroes" treat the bigger kids in my neighborhood like their enemies—beating them, harassing them, using racial slurs, violating them without cause. These weren't criminals; they were kids. My heroes were the ones causing the harm. In that moment, the badge lost its shine. The illusion cracked. Then, on my fifteenth birthday, I was assaulted by two cops who bashed my head against a phone booth in the city of Bell Gardens. I was forced to stand against a wall, and my picture was taken—which was common practice by police officers at that time, even when dealing with children—and the racial slurs never left my ears. At that point, the illusion was completely shattered.

I learned early that looks are deceiving.

But it didn't stop at cops. At an early age, even before my violent encounter with the police, I had started noticing the same pattern in almost everyone around me. Churchgoers preached love on Sunday but were the greatest sinners and monsters at home and in the community. Teachers talked about hope but were fueled by bitterness. So many preachers, activists, and politicians—even relatives and close family friends—were pretending, smiling in public but broken in private. The lie wasn't always in what they said; it was often in their actions. Even some parents I knew were pretending to be parents.

The older I got, the more I saw that many people wore labels they hadn't earned. They claimed loyalty, wisdom, honor, or goodness without living it. Alcohol would bring out their true selves—the affectionate hugs would turn into slurred insults, the warm smiles replaced by anger—or sometimes it was the opposite. I learned then that lying isn't always verbal; sometimes it's how you show up.

Just when I was losing trust in everything, I heard words that pulled me in: "Nigga, we real."

These words came from a new group—the gangsters, the street dudes, the free spirits of the city. These weren't the suit-and-tie types. They didn't answer to anyone. They spoke raw, acted bold, and lived unfiltered. There was no pretending. You either wore red or wore blue. You were either a street dude or a schoolboy. You lived a life of crime or you didn't. These individuals seemed to be what they claimed to be.

It looked real, so I believed it. I believed that "people who look street will be street." I had no reason not to. It matched what I saw and what I hoped for. The myth felt real because I had so little else to believe in.

But as I got older, more involved, and deeper into the streets, that belief began to break down. I started realizing that people entered street life for different reasons. Some did it to fit in. Some out of fear. Some because of peer pressure. Others were spoiled kids rebelling against structure. Some were escaping abusive homes, looking for love in the only place that felt familiar. Others were following behind family already knee-deep in a life of crime. And some were just chameleons, pretending, playing street because it gave them protection, attention, and a sense of power.

That's when I began to notice a whole other class of people—the fakes I once couldn't see, the ones who were so good at pretending that they had even fooled the "real ones." They threw rocks and hid their hands. They were scam artists, storytellers, clout chasers. They built names off things they never did, and rode the coattails of those who were proven solid. They wore gang attire like a costume, selling an image to those who didn't know any better—especially the younger kids, who often copied what they saw, sometimes with tragic results.

These people were not street. They were actors, and their performances had consequences.

Some were exposed and became known as "hood rejects." Others slipped through the cracks because playing their roles well—some even carried guns—but would never have the courage to use them. I used to get mad at them for taking advantage of a world I thought was sacred to me. Over time, I learned to respect the hustle because surviving off charisma and illusion in a world where bullets fly and reputations get checked every day takes talent. It's a dangerous game. But still, it's a game played well. And trying to protect the streets from them is a fool's errand.

Some of these people were so committed to the act that they carried it into prison, thinking the role would keep working there too. But that's where the mask falls off. In prison, your role can be tested daily. Gang riots, racial politics, confrontation with COs, beef with your cellmate, or even beef with people in your own crew—those are real-time tests. That's when the line between actor and participant gets erased and people start saying, "I see something in this nigga that don't add up."

Eventually, the truth comes out.

Street life has levels. It has roles. It has lanes. And those who don't stay in their lane usually get exposed. Some of the most seasoned gangsters forget that many around them are camouflaged, hiding their truth, selling an image, not revealing what's real. And when you don't check what's real, you become part of the myth.

I've seen it happen. For example, I had a homie get seven years in prison for shooting a so-called gangster, who himself was a known shooter. He had the look, the reputation, even the background that everyone feared, but when the tables turned, he snitched. Another friend got nine years for pistol-whipping a man in front of his family, thinking he was dealing with a street soldier. That man testified. A homegirl of mine got thirty-plus years for shooting someone who everyone thought lived by the same code. But that "gangster" came to court in a suit, sat on the stand, and pointed her out as the woman who shot him. And a childhood friend of mine got life in prison for avenging his cousin—a supposed gangster who didn't have the guts to defend himself even when his own life was on the line.

Those stories? That's the reality behind the myth. These people acted like gangsters when it mattered, but they paid the price because the people they trusted to do the same were only playing street. And some of them—my people—are still doing time behind that betrayal.

The myth says "people who look street will be street," but the truth is that looks don't measure loyalty, depth, courage, or conviction. Real street life isn't about outfits or lingo; it's about the invisible weight you carry. It's your past, your trauma, your values, your pain, your future, and how you respond when the pressure hits. It's not the tattoo—it's what the tattoo means when it's challenged. It's what the tattoo covers: you.

Sure, there are people who look the part and are the part. But even that's hard to prove now. Tattoos became makeup. The street persona became commercial. Silence became optional.

And when the real moments come—whether in a prison yard or a dark alley—that's when the truth is visible.

Not everyone who "looks street" is about that life. And not everyone who is about that life wants to stay in it.

That's what the myth never tells you. Looking the part doesn't mean you are the part; it just means you're a target. And when people decide to come for that bull's-eye, your costume won't save you.

The streets don't care if you're pretending. The system doesn't either. Neither one cares if you're confused, unloved, lost, or in the middle of changing. They only care about whether you get caught slipping when you're out committing crimes or what they can bleed from you.

And I've watched too many people pay the ultimate price for trying to live up to an image they never believed in—or failed to walk away from in time.

In this world, what you present is what you are. As the saying goes, "first impressions are everything." Impressions last. Once you've claimed a certain look, role, or affiliation, people expect you to fulfill it. To act it out. To prove it daily.

The streets make it dangerous to want the perks—the protection, the hood fame, the money, the women, the fake loyalty—without the price. Because eventually somebody's going to ask, "What have you done for us lately?" And if your answer ain't good enough, you're a leech, a parasite, a fugazi-ass nigga who needs to be thrown away—or worse.

What people see is what they judge. That's what makes this myth so dangerous. The streets are visual, but survival goes deeper than that. It's a psychological game built on strategy, emotional control, and adaptability. It's about knowing when and how to say "cool, I'm wit it" or "get the fuck outta my face." Survival doesn't come from how you look—it comes from how you think and how you react to life and its challenges.

THE TRUTH

Street life encompasses anything and everything imaginable. Falsehoods, poseurs, and perpetrators are all equally part of the makeup, complexities, dilemmas, harsh survival, and deadly realities that street life offers. Those who appear the toughest have, at times, been found to be the weakest. But through their great performance, they acquired the greatest following. Not every person who itches to be seen as a gangster wants to be treated as such, and behind closed doors, many of them are everything that they claim not to be.

LOOKING STREET ISN'T STREET.

MYTH 16

REAL NIGGAS RUN THE STREETS

> Real niggas keep it 100, they stand on business, they don't bend or fold or crumble fa nobody. They get nothing but love cause they real in the streets. Lil homies wanna be like'm. They never compromise. They never back down. They move shit; shit don't move them. That's why they run the streets.

There has long been a belief in the streets that some individuals hold absolute power, a near-mythical status as untouchables who control many parts of the underworld. But this belief is rooted in illusion, and the younger the believer, the greater the hold this myth has on the mind. The streets, much like nature itself, truly cannot be ruled; it is an untamed force as destructive and indifferent as a tornado, earthquake, or hurricane. Those who think they control the streets inevitably discover that the streets cannot be controlled—they erupt like a volcano, consuming anyone who underestimates their volatility.

> "The world is a spiritual vessel and cannot be controlled. Those who control, fail. Those who grasp lose."
>
> —LAO TZU, *TAO TE CHING*

At its core, the myth hinges on what it means to "run the streets," which can mean staying awake until sunrise, sometimes roaming aimlessly, or having a relentless hustle to accumulate the trappings of success—sex, money, cars, and clothes. In this context, "running the streets" is synonymous with having ultimate control, power, and influence—embodying dominance, delegating authority, and having mastery over the unpredictable forces of street life.

The pursuit of this control often revolves around the holy trinity of street life: money, power, and respect. Of these, power stands as the most seductive and dangerous. It whispers promises of invincibility, feeding your ego until you feel immortal—a god who bends the world to his or her own will. But history has repeatedly shattered this illusion. The names of once-revered street figures—John Gotti, Big Meech, El Chapo, Stanley "Tookie" Williams, Pablo Escobar—now serve as cautionary tales. Each rose to power projecting the image of being untouchable, only to face defeat, imprisonment, or death. Many others, whose names are now forgotten, forever lost to the pages of street history, met similar fates in the midst of the chaos they believed they controlled. As Stanley "Tookie" Williams, co-founder of the Crips, once reflected, starting the Crips was a response to violence with the intention of protecting his own community from other gangs, but he later noticed that his actions eventually intensified the very violence he sought to defend against, only making matters worse.

This same cycle also consumes others, because "niggas" in the streets can't see the future when they first begin, which brings us to the term *nigga* itself—an ambiguous and controversial word that shifts meaning depending on context. It can be synonymous with many other words, such as *friend*, *idiot*, or *dude*. *Nigga* exists as part of a dialect (sometimes called Ebonics), and even before the rise of urban street culture, some tried to soften or reframe the word as its roots are in the word *nigger*—undeniably a racial slur. While historically and tragically tied to men and women of African descent, in street life the dialectal use of *nigga* has transcended race, age, nationality, and even social class, functioning as a term of endearment, camaraderie, or insult depending on tone and intent.

A "real nigga," however, is something more—a concept tied to identity, loyalty, and reputation, and the term is sometimes used deceptively to hype or encourage others to be cool or stay friendly. But here, to be a "real nigga" in the streets is to adhere to an unspoken code: staying true to principles, never betraying values, and embodying the street's ideals of strength and authenticity.

But this identity is not static; it's fluid. With each generation, the meaning of what being a "real nigga" is evolves, shaped by newcomers and their newfound perceptions. At its heart, though, it remains tied to a deep-seated loyalty to street life and its so-called rules—a commitment that often leaves little room for regret or escape.

Yet even this loyalty does not shield the streets from outside influence. Ironically, those who claim to "run the streets" can become manipulated by forces far greater than they are. Outsiders, including law enforcement and government agencies, whether corrupted or not, have long played puppet masters in the streets. Through the quiet distribution of guns and drugs, these institutions or lone wolves amplify the chaos many see in street life, all the while pulling strings to maintain control, cooperation, and betrayal. Manipulation acts as a currency of power, forcing street figures into a perpetual tug-of-war for survival.

One example was Operation Fast and Furious, "a high-profile scandal that ensnared former President Barack Obama's Justice Department, the ATF, and ex-Attorney General Eric Holder. The imbroglio saw federal agents allow more than two thousand firearms to be sold illegally to known or suspected straw purchasers. At the time, the federal government hoped the weapons could be used to track and ultimately arrest the high-ranking leaders of Mexican drug cartels. The sting operation backfired, however, with the guns being used to facilitate crimes along the US-Mexico border. The scandal came to light in 2011, shortly after two firearms involved in the sting were found at a crime scene where a US Border Patrol agent had been killed.

This tug-of-war is no less destructive than a battlefield. Bombs may not be dropped, but lives are destroyed, communities are torn apart, and dreams are crushed. In most cases, these neighborhoods take many years to be rebuilt—if they are ever rebuilt at all. The myth of untouchability dissolves as "real niggas" confront the reality of these external forces. Their perceived dominance, whether achieved through aggression or the drug trade, is revealed to be smoke and mirrors, a fragile illusion shattered by the manipulative hands of those who control the larger game.

Law enforcement demands participation in an intricate dance of survival. City, state, and federal enforcers fine-tune the rhythm, expecting the streets to move to their beat. The "real niggas" who refuse to dance—choosing independence or resistance—find themselves with longer prison sentences, cut off from the public, or even sentenced to death. Nevertheless, the streets are filled with overly ambitious characters—priced cheap—hoping to be labeled a "real nigga" at any cost. George Jung, one of America's most infamous drug traffickers, came to realize that his ambition far outweighed his talent. Many will come to realize the same, and as he did, most will probably recognize it too late.

In the end, the streets are not something to be conquered. They are a force that humbles even the most powerful, reminding all who dare to claim dominion that the streets are neither loyal nor forgiving. To believe otherwise is to buy into the myth—a costly delusion that will lead to an inevitable downfall.

STREET VIEW

While growing up, I saw street dudes as the rawest form of men, the embodiment of unfiltered human nature. They seemed to be carving their existence into a society that cloaked its own violence, hatred, and greed behind a facade of civility. Street dudes rejected that facade entirely. They moved with an air of defiance, untouched by conventional rules and driven by a code that, from their own perspective, demanded survival, respect, and power.

Even in death, these individuals—in the many neighborhoods I grew up in—lived on as legends. Their names were tattooed on bodies, spray-painted on walls, and immortalized in stories passed down, sometimes through generations and usually told with reverence. Faces adorned T-shirts as symbols of remembrance, and their deaths were marked with rituals like pouring out liquor for "the dead homies." But these moments of respect often spiraled into cycles of revenge, spilling more blood and solidifying the belief that these men or women did not die in vain. To me, this painted the streets as a battleground where only the strongest thrived and where "real niggas" ruled, and you could only know this based on who the last man standing was and who was most feared. Some ruled with an iron fist, while others came off as relaxed, understanding, cool, and patient.

The allure of these men (and even the occasional woman) was irresistible, suggesting that street life offered freedom from societal rules. These individuals faced life-threatening challenges with unrelenting willpower, commanding respect and confronting any force that dared oppose them, including the law. Watching them reject police brutality and scorn contempt from others solidified my belief that the streets belonged to "real niggas" and that their power was unmatched, even by the so-called unstoppable system of law enforcement.

But then came the paradox that I eventually had to come to grips with: what happens when an unstoppable force collides with an immovable object? This ancient philosophical metaphor perfectly framed the tension between the streets and the system. Street dudes are seen as the immovable, unyielding rulers of their domains. Law enforcement, by contrast, represents the unstoppable force—the enforcers of order, constantly pushing against the chaos of the streets. When these two forces met, they appeared to be clashing—but they were merely reshaping each other.

The streets and the system left their marks on one another. Law enforcement, once the epitome of control and justice, was not immune to the influence of the streets. Officers and lawmakers were often seduced by the same forces they were tasked with dismantling—money, power, sex, and respect. Many succumbed to corruption, taking bribes, turning a blind eye, or even participating in the very crimes they were sworn to stop. Others lost their moral compass entirely, using their positions to exploit, oppress, or abuse, further blurring the line between justice and tyranny.

Many of these acts of corruption remain hidden, with those involved retiring as so-called heroes, celebrated for their service and shielded from accountability. This duality—that righteousness can coexist with wickedness—reveals a harsh truth: law and morality are only as strong as the individuals who create or enforce them. When the enforcers themselves become tainted, the shattered illusion of an unstoppable system proves it was not what it claimed to be.

On the other side, the immovable street figures I once adored also shifted. Under pressure from the system, some "real niggas" became informants or snitches, betraying the codes to save themselves. Others walked away from the streets entirely, broken or transformed by the weight of their pasts. These shifts revealed to me another uncomfortable truth: power is not absolute. The quest to dominate—to run the streets—leads not to freedom but to entanglement in deeper cycles of contradictions and moral decay.

The myth that "real niggas running the streets" suggests an untouchable dominance, but the reality I learned was far more complex. The streets and the modern system will forever be locked in an endless dance in which each reshapes the other, blurring the lines between power and weakness, hero and villain, good and bad, right and wrong.

Even Donald Trump, in 2018, echoed this dance on national television. While serving as president of the United States, he famously condemned "flipping," a term used in and out of the streets, meaning working with law enforcement to take down criminals. Trump stated, "It should probably be illegal." In 2024 he was reelected to the highest office of the land, which represents that same law and justice that claims to be "the unstoppable force." His words mirrored the G Code of loyalty and disdain for betrayal, illustrating how the struggle over trust and power transcends environments. True power, it seems, isn't about running the streets; it's about breaking free from the forces that try to define and control us—whether that's the streets, the system, or the myths we cling to.

> **THE TRUTH**
>
> While it may appear that "real niggas" run the streets, the truth is that no one holds absolute power. The streets are not controlled by individuals but by the cycles of violence, betrayal, and survival that consume everyone involved, including innocent bystanders. Those who may seem untouchable can be brought down, whether by law enforcement, betrayal from within, or the inevitable consequences of life. Power in the streets is fleeting and often a facade, as the game itself is rigged and no one is truly immune.

THE STREETS ARE NOT CONTROLLABLE.

──── MYTH 17 ────

IF YOU RESPECT THE GAME, THE GAME WILL RESPECT YOU

> If you respect the game, the game will respect you because honor is a two-way street in street life. Real ones don't disrespect others for nothing. So if you show respect, you'll receive it in return. When people respect you, you create a bond that shields you from betrayal and harm, ensuring others will honor your respect and support you, as you do them.

This myth is often taught early in street life as a guiding principle, but its application is far from straightforward. That's because "the game" itself isn't one unified path—it's a layered world with many lanes.

The game is a popular term often used interchangeably with *street culture* or *street life*. But within the culture, there are subcultures—each with its own identity, rules, and hustle. Pimping, robbing, gangbanging, gun running, prostitution, drug dealing, scamming, fraud—each one is considered its own version of "the game," and the common denominator is the thrill: money, cars, clothes, sex, power, and of course, respect.

But the term *the game* is polysemous—it doesn't just belong to the streets. It also applies to more "legit" arenas: sports, politics, the music business, and even the so-called game of life. What all these "games" have in common is one central idea: competition. At the heart of that competition is one rule: win. The game is a system in itself, and it doesn't take sides, so how "winning" is defined is up to the individual player. Aristotle Onassis, a businessman who built the world's largest shipping fleet, once said, "I have no friends and no enemies—only competitors."

Because of this competitive nature, players tend to form groups—gangs, crews, cliques, hoods, or business teams—to increase their chances of survival or success. These groups often establish their own rules—some written, some unwritten, some spoken, some simply understood. Within those rules, one idea tends to sit near the top: respect the game, and it will respect you—or to put it more simply, show respect to get respect.

But this is a romanticized notion, which is why the myth becomes dangerous. The game, whether street or professional, doesn't actually care about respect—it rewards outcomes. And when survival or status is on the line, many people will break their own codes. That's when the illusion of mutual respect crumbles.

This is why respect in street life is not always reciprocal or unconditional, even though it's a widely repeated mantra, perhaps out of hope or expectation. While many will still elevate this myth as an undeniable fact, it operates within a complex, shifting system of values and perceptions. It's often mistaken for an all-access pass to navigate the underworld safely, but the reality is much more unpredictable and dangerous.

Respect has layers and nuances. For example, you might respect someone for their loyalty but not for their personal choices, or vice versa. Similarly, someone might hold you in high regard in one aspect but still disrespect you in another. In the volatile environment of street life, these conflicting layers can lead to confusion and tension, with respect being withheld, revoked, or weaponized depending on the situation. For instance, a person's many admirable traits might still fail to outweigh a single action that provokes disrespect, leading to conflict or betrayal.

This dynamic makes the myth particularly dangerous. Openly showing respect—by recognizing boundaries, being polite, or treating others equally—can sometimes be perceived as weakness. In the streets, where survival often requires dominance or aggression, such gestures may be treated with contempt. Force and assertiveness are often seen as the only reliable ways to "earn respect," but these approaches carry risks. Aggression may earn fear or camaraderie, but it also invites competition and retaliation. Self-proclaimed "alpha males" in street life often feel compelled to undermine those they once respected, using betrayal, violence, or even murder to assert dominance or maintain their position in a precarious hierarchy. For some, being second best is simply not an option.

Yet respect isn't always what it seems in the streets; it can be wielded as a strategic tool. Feigned respect is often used to manipulate or deceive, much like a Trojan horse. Take the example of *Fresh*, a film in which the protagonist, a twelve-year-old boy navigating the dangers of New York street life, uses calculated displays of respect to gain trust from those around him. His strategic manipulation of respect becomes a means to protect himself and free his older sister from their toxic environment. This highlights how respect, rather than being a sincere exchange, can become a weapon or a survival strategy.

This duality makes respect in street life hard to trust. The outward gestures may seem genuine, but the underlying motives often reflect self-preservation, opportunism, or deception. This dynamic reveals the hollowness of the myth, as respect becomes less about mutual regard and more about survival in a cutthroat world.

Adding to the complexity is the distinction between *giving respect* and *being respectful*. These terms are often conflated but represent fundamentally different concepts:

- **Having/Giving Respect:** This is an active acknowledgment of someone's qualities, status, or achievements. It's often earned or situational, directed at individuals based on their behavior or accomplishments. For instance, showing deference to a mentor or someone in authority shows respect.
- **Being Respectful:** This is a consistent behavior that reflects general decency, politeness, and regard for others regardless of their status or actions. It's about maintaining a respectful attitude as a personal or professional trait, not necessarily tied to the other person's merit. Holding the door open or refraining from interrupting someone are examples of being respectful.

In street life or life in general, these distinctions blur, creating even more uncertainty. Giving respect is often seen as conditional, while being respectful can be misinterpreted as weakness or vulnerability. This leaves individuals constantly navigating a treacherous path, where even small missteps can have severe consequences.

Ultimately, showing respect can be a form of letting your guard down, so the myth that you are guaranteed respect by showing it to others fails to account for the complexities of human behavior, particularly in the unpredictable and often ruthless realm of street life. Respect, in this context, is not a reciprocal contract but a fluid and volatile concept shaped by survival, perception, and power dynamics.

"There can be no covenants between men and lions, wolves and lambs can never be of one mind, but hate each other out and out and through."

—HOMER

STREET VIEW

The concept of respect carries immense weight. Across cultures, social hierarchies, and personal relationships, respect is something people strive for, demand, or use as currency. Yet in my experience—especially within street life—respect isn't always reciprocal. It's a lesson I learned the hard way, through betrayals from friends, strangers, and even family.

I've given respect generously, only to find that I was ridiculed behind my back. I've helped others in their darkest moments, offering financial or emotional support, only to discover they were secretly plotting against me. I've cheered for people's dreams and goals, only to learn that they were wishing and waiting for my downfall. These experiences darkened my perspective on respect, making me cautious and even hesitant to extend it. But my curiosity made me ponder what respect really was.

For example, I had many associates in street life. When I look back now, I realize I may have foolishly called some of them friends. Because I believed in the code of the streets, I extended my friendship with respect, assuming that if I stayed true to the code and always showed respect, the bond would never break.

But when money was involved and their money got low and their hunger for it grew, jealousy crept in like a gray cloud hanging over us. Suddenly, everything was up for grabs. Respect became blurry, and the idea of friendship meant nothing. One of those so-called friends—someone I once referred to as my best friend—tried to take my life in a planned robbery. I had to open fire with my own gun, and luckily, I only wounded my friend, hitting him in the abdomen.

While I was also lucky enough to get in the car and drive away, the event left me heartbroken, confused, and questioning why respect mattered so much. Was it simply a social expectation to maintain order that gave society its civility? A selfish craving to feel valued or powerful? Or perhaps a way to affirm our place in a chaotic world? Growing up, I was taught that respect among street dudes or people in general was sacred—an unwritten law. But life taught me that respect is fragile and conditional, a romanticized notion. It doesn't always resolve conflicts or create or keep peace. Strangely enough, I found that disrespect sometimes worked better.

Disrespect operates on fear. It's a power play, an act of dominance that keeps others in check and docile. When someone is publicly humiliated or disrespected, it serves as a warning to others: "This could happen to you." This tactic, I've seen throughout my time in street life, demands attention, evokes fear, and even inspires admiration among those who are drawn to chaos and unpredictability. Disrespect works because it disrupts norms and projects power, bending rules and making others question their own boundaries and even their own purpose.

But the cost of disrespect is steep. I've seen many fire back at others, and in some cases the consequence for those who were disrespectful was losing their life. Disrespect fuels individualism, mistrust, and the survivalist mentality of "every person for themselves." It erodes any hope for unity, deepens divides, and reinforces the cycles of fear and aggression that dominate communities entrenched in street life. Once respect is lost, it becomes harder to rebuild trust or foster cooperation. Entire neighborhoods fall into chaos, fear outweighs hope, and isolation becomes the norm.

Respect was once a word brimming with substance, or so I thought, but it has been weakened by human ambition. It's buried under the weight of greed, power struggles, and self-interest. Over time, its meaning has been hollowed out. People mislead, manipulate, and betray without shame or accountability. What remains is a principle that's rarely lived out in full—a word that feels more like a myth than a reality.

In street life, this dynamic became even more pronounced. I started to see that respect is transactional, a negotiable asset traded for survival, status, or convenience. It's not given freely or earned through virtue alone; it's bought, sold, or stolen by aggression. And even when earned, it's fragile—as fleeting as a good reputation tainted by a single act of betrayal.

This myth—"if you respect the game, the game will respect you"—rests on the false hope that respect is a mutual exchange. The reality is far more complex. Respect demands consistency, trust, accountability, and even a guarantee, but in environments shaped by power dynamics, it's often replaced by fear and opportunism. To navigate these spaces, I learned, one must not only give respect but also understand its limits and vulnerabilities.

Ultimately, the pursuit of respect should be about balance.

While we may not always see it returned, respect still holds value: it's a reflection of who we are, what we can be, and what we stand for. But in the harsh realities of life—in this case, street life—it's naive to believe that respect guarantees respect in return. Instead, it's a choice we make, knowing full well the risks and consequences that come with it.

> **THE TRUTH**
>
> Respect doesn't guarantee loyalty, protection, or honesty. It's often taken for granted, misunderstood, or exploited by those who value self-interest over mutual regard. In some environments, showing respect can expose vulnerabilities rather than ensure reciprocity. Even enemies show each other respect or are respectful, but that doesn't mean they aren't plotting an attack.

RESPECT IS A TOOL IN STREET LIFE, NOT A PROMISE THAT THE GAME ABIDES BY.

———— MYTH 18 ————

YOU CAN'T BUY RESPECT

> Respect must be earned and is always rooted in sincerity, character, and mutual understanding. Respect cannot be bought or traded like material possessions; it is a reflection of genuine regard for someone's values and actions. Respect is the only real thing left in the streets.

The idea that respect can't be bought is a romanticized notion, especially in the streets, where power and influence often hold more weight than ideals. People say, "Don't give your respect away—make others earn it." So we must ask, if respect can be given freely without being earned, why can't it be bought? And if it can be earned, why can't it be sold? These contradictions expose the fragile logic beneath this widely accepted belief.

Many myths like this are rooted in the *illusory truth effect*—a psychological phenomenon in which repeated exposure to a statement, even if it's false, leads people to accept it as true without questioning its origins or evidence. The myth "you can't buy respect" thrives because it's echoed in street teachings, rap music, and social norms. Its frequent repetition grants it an air of legitimacy despite evidence to the contrary.

In environments shaped by survival and status, respect operates like any other commodity. It is negotiated, traded, sold for a price, and sometimes foolishly given away. Those with money or power can often manipulate how others perceive and treat them. In such contexts, respect is less an intangible moral ideal and more a currency that reflects leverage. And yet people rarely question "earned" respect, even though arrogance stemming from it has cost people far more than what could have been paid for respect outright. The myth collapses when people recognize that respect is as much about perception as reality—it is fluid and conditional rather than absolute.

> "Things are not always what they seem; the first appearance deceives many; the intelligence of a few perceives what has been carefully hidden."
>
> —PHAEDRUS

Think of respect as a gun: a powerful tool that not everyone can legally possess. On the streets, respect, like a gun, is bought and sold on the black market. A person who acquires a gun legally may gain an air of legitimacy, while someone who gets one illegally might conceal it in shame. In both cases, possession of the gun—or respect—grants a certain power, but the means of acquisition can alter its perception.

Still, when people argue that respect can't be bought, they often imagine a direct, hand-to-hand cash exchange—someone sliding over a stack of money and demanding to be respected. That literal view becomes some people's main focus, as if the concept of buying respect only applies in obvious, transactional ways. But that argument falls short because it misunderstands how respect often works.

Consider this: a stranger walks up and gives someone in need $5,000, no strings attached. The money, combined with the gesture, triggers a feeling in the receiver: admiration, appreciation, maybe even gratitude. That emotional response is, by definition, a form of respect. The stranger will, more than likely, leave a long-lasting impression on the receiver. And here's the catch: you can't always dictate how others feel, but you can influence it. That's the hidden transaction.

Money is tied to the most basic human needs—food, shelter, safety, water, clothing, education—it is how those things are commonly acquired. It's also symbolic of the nonessentials of life—alcohol, partying, luxurious vacations. All of these things produce feelings of relief, satisfaction, and emotional warmth. So when someone provides the means to access those things, we instinctively associate them with power, value, and worthiness. We start to see them as someone to admire and respect, even if just for a moment, and here we can see the lines blur between manipulation and human nature.

So the idea that respect can't be bought isn't as airtight as many think. Money has always had the power to move people—and what moves us often earns our respect.

The antiquated idea that people have "sold their souls," bought etiquette, paid for love, negotiated their dignity, or even bought friends is widely accepted in literature, music, and culture. Yet street life resists the notion that respect can be transactional or purchased, clinging to the belief that respect is earned through character or integrity alone. This resistance stems from a near-mythical belief in respect as an incorruptible force. But in practice, respect functions as a tool of survival and manipulation, across all lifestyles.

Respect, like power or loyalty, is dynamic and conditional. For example, a drug dealer might feign respect for a rival to avoid unnecessary conflict, while secretly planning their downfall. Similarly, someone might "pay" for respect by hiring muscle, flaunting wealth, or committing acts of violence to secure their status. These actions blur the lines between earned respect and its performative or transactional forms.

This duality raises questions: when respect is bought, forced, or strategically given, is it truly respect? Or is it compliance, fear, or opportunism disguised as admiration? This ambiguity explains why respect, particularly in street life, often feels insincere. It is a means to an end—spent, traded, or discarded as easily as money or loyalty.

These complexities are further explored in the previous myth, "if you respect the game, the game will respect you," which highlights the fragility of respect in environments driven by power dynamics. It challenges the assumption that respect is automatically reciprocal, exposing how it is often shown strategically, not out of genuine admiration. The transactional nature of respect means that even when offered, it is rarely, if ever, unconditional. What many call "real" or "true" respect is often a romanticized ideal—used to maintain order within a culture. In reality, respect is shaped by hierarchies and institutions to keep people aligned with shared interests—whether that be stability, security, or prosperity. It shows honor, but in the end it produces order—this is why we are raised to offer respect to people we don't know.

Ultimately, street life and life in general have made the idea of selling one's respect so reprehensible that very few would openly admit to having sold their respect at one time or another. But understanding respect as a commodity dismantles the myth that it can't be bought. Respect is not an immutable principle but a negotiable tool of leverage, shaped by survival and manipulation. While people may cling to the romanticized notion of respect as noble and incorruptible, the realities of life—on the streets and beyond—reveal a far more volatile and transactional truth.

As I've always said, "In a capitalist society, everything is negotiable," which only leaves the question: do you want to negotiate?

STREET VIEW

As a child encountering many adults—those in street life and those outside of it—I was always taught to never give my respect away. "Make people earn it," they said. Respect, I was told, had to be rooted in character, mutual understanding, and authenticity. Sometimes it would have to be taken—in other words, beaten into someone. This belief was even echoed in American pop culture. For a while, I believed it. Even as I grew older, getting deeper into street life, that myth was constantly repeated: "You can't buy respect."

But when I started looking closer—at real interactions, real situations—I saw something different. The line between earned respect and transactional respect wasn't just blurry; it was often invisible.

I watched people earn respect not for their integrity, but for their willingness to hurt others or the fear they could instill just by walking into a room. In some cases, respect was just survival. People showed it not out of admiration, but because they didn't want to be next in line for punishment. As Albert Camus believed, respect based on fear is despicable. Still, in the streets, some people found ways to live with that contradiction. They weren't confrontational, so they played the game, offering respect to those they feared because it felt safer than the alternative.

Look at the characters Deebo and Big Worm from *Friday*. Other characters in the movie showed them respect, even honored them—not because of who they were as people, but because of the harm they could cause. This is not far from reality. This is the reality I grew up in.

In the streets—or in life, period—people go where they feel safest, most protected, or most rewarded. That means respect often follows money, power, or popularity. People respected what they could get from someone: a place to belong, access to opportunity, or even just protection. I saw it time and time again—someone would pull up in a flashy car, flex some muscle, pass out a few dollars, and instantly they were surrounded by people who "respected" them, not for who they were, but for what they had. Sometimes those people would go so far as to defend the "respected" person in their absence, hoping to maintain that one-sided relationship.

Money bought respect all the time—it just wore different outfits. In circles where someone refused to play along, they often found themselves ostracized or forced to defend why they didn't bow down and "kiss the ring." Not everyone is easily bought, but in a world where survival often depends on alliances, "playing along" was sometimes the easiest route and in most cases the best choice.

But for me, it was the hardest choice. I couldn't pretend to like someone without first knowing who they really were, and that lack of talent cost me. I asked too many questions, and in most circles questions are treated as the enemy of progress. To many, a question feels like peeling back layers they would rather keep hidden. Most people prefer their disguise left untouched, unchallenged, and unquestioned.

Many people confused respect with reward. They began to associate someone who could offer a "good time" or material benefits with respectability. Others went along for the ride, playing friendly just to benefit from the situation—privately holding disdain, but publicly offering praise. It was a means to survive, a hustle, a tactic.

On the streets, the word *respect* became romanticized—just like *love, loyalty, gangster,* and even *going federal.* People used it freely but rarely understood what they were really saying. Many didn't even realize they were buying or selling it.

But those who did? They knew the game. They knew respect could be as thin as paper. That's why many kept a gun—they understood that the same people who once showed them respect might "try them" later—meaning test their gangster, or harm them. In the streets, respect can be bought, but more often it's rented or leased. And just like that, when the contract ends, people will "try their hand" at taking what's yours—your money, your woman, or your life.

I started seeing respect for what it really was: transactional. It's like a doorman. He opens the door for us and greets us with courtesy. On the surface, this seems like respect, but it's really a paid service—he's doing what he's compensated to do, and his actions are rooted in obligation, not reverence.

In the streets, I started to see that this same principle plays out on a larger scale: money, influence, loyalty, and even fear all have some properties of respect. The difference between so-called genuine respect and the kind bought with power or wealth can be hard to distinguish, especially when both result in outward displays of reverence. Just like the doorman who opens the door out of duty, people can show respect because it's expected or because it's incentivized.

This started to challenge my romanticized notion that

respect can't be bought. In reality, especially on the streets, respect is often as transactional as any other form of social currency. People will trade respect for money, security, or status if the circumstances are right, revealing the deeper truth that respect, like most things, has a price in the right context.

I would have this debate with many street affiliates, including acquaintances and close friends. No matter who I was talking to or who we were in front of, I didn't hold any punches in making my point. They would argue that earned respect is never fleeting, unlike negotiated respect. Some would say, "My nigga, if the money leaves, then the respect goes, so clearly, that shit ain't real respect," assuming this proves their point that paid or transactional respect is not "real respect." I found myself arguing against their point by stating, "If earned respect is genuine, like a father who is known to work hard and provide for his family, then assume he lost his job and is unable to provide for his family in the same way. The respect toward him would not be lost. But for many, it is. Some of us, maybe even including his wife and children, will lose respect for him immediately, and for others the respect will diminish slowly." We can respect people for what they used to be, but what really matters is who or what they are in the moment.

I extended my point by saying, "OK, my nigga, let's use Sammy the Bull for an example. If people really respected Sammy before he became a rat nigga, then by their own logic, they wouldn't stop respecting him after he became a snitch. After all, if respect is based on trusting someone's judgment, then his decision to become a rat nigga must be seen as just another one of his right decisions. But of course, you and I know that's not what happened—people's respect for him vanished the moment he stopped giving them what they wanted, or even being what they wanted him to be. My point, again, is that respect is always conditional, tied to circumstances and outcomes, making it far more transactional than many of y'all are willing to admit."

But of course many still argued that respect must be genuine to have "real" value. I would say, "If that's the case, can any display of so-called genuine respect truly be trusted? How would you know? People often play the long game—showing respect for years, not out of sincerity, but to secure something down the line, like access to an inheritance after someone's death, or something immediate, like being respectful to a woman so you can fuck. Right?" When respect or its appearance can be sustained for personal gain, the line between genuine and transactional respect blurs, casting doubt on the authenticity of all respect. As we say in the streets, "I don't know what this nigga is up to."

Now, some may call this view cynical, but to that, I say you're gullible or even egotistical, especially in street life. If you believe respect is always pure and given because of who you are, you're ignoring the realities of human motives and our ambition. Respect often comes at a price, even if it's not immediately obvious.

THE TRUTH

Respect is rarely the pure, earned ideal we imagine. It's a currency that shifts with power, influence, and opportunity. Whether through wealth, status, or fear, respect can be bought, sold, or negotiated, even when we convince ourselves that the respect we receive or show is sincere. Like any commodity, it's subject to the forces of leverage—what we think of as "genuine" respect often dissolves the moment someone's actions no longer serve or please us. In truth, respect is less about character and more about what we have to offer, even if we are offering good character.

RESPECT IS A CURRENCY THAT SHIFTS WITH POWER, INFLUENCE, AND OPPORTUNITY.

MYTH 19

TRUST NO ONE

> Trust makes a man gullible, and as a fool, he'll be the first clown to be played. Everyone's a criminal, and criminals prove that they can't be trusted, so trusting no one is the only way to move in life. You can't even trust yo homies cause them fools grimy. Sometimes you can't even trust yourself.

"Trust no one" echoes a primal instinct, both inside and outside of street life. Even in some of the supposedly best homes and communities, parents often tell their children, "Don't trust strangers." "Don't trust everyone." "Don't trust certain races of people." And sometimes even "Don't trust all family members or friends." Yet, ironically, strangers and some of those same family members and friends still end up in those homes. That's often an individual's first encounter with the dangers and contradictions of the no-trust mindset.

Street life mirrors this confusion. It's a world shaped by betrayal, survival, and violence, so distrust becomes a reflex.

In earlier myths, like "once solid, always solid" and "family is always loyal," trust has already been tested and sometimes shattered—by friends, by partners, even by blood. "Always" rarely lives up to its name in the streets.

But this myth goes deeper. It doesn't just say trust is risky; it says trust is impossible. And while that belief may feel true, it's one of the most damaging lies that street life teaches.

It makes sense that it feels true—trust is vulnerability, a crack in one's defenses that invites exploitation, manipulation, or destruction. In street life or even life in general, where survival is often portrayed as a zero-sum game, trust can feel like a liability, a dangerous leap of faith in a world where self-interest reigns supreme. Those who adopt this mantra—"trust no one"—often convince themselves that isolation ensures protection and that self-reliance is the only true safeguard.

Yet this myth overlooks a critical truth: no one survives alone. Trust is not a luxury; it's a necessary part of life. Every human interaction, whether in the streets, the workplace, or the home, depends on some level of trust. As philosopher Onora O'Neill has argued, individuals and institutions alike rely on the belief that others will act as they claim they will—and that we, in turn, will do the same. Without that basic expectation, society would break down and we truly couldn't survive. Even in the grittiest corners of street life, trust remains a silent contract, trying to hold things together.

For example, consider drug dealers: they must trust that their supplier won't sell them a bad product. They also have to trust that their buyers won't rob them or become informants or police agents. Robbers must trust that their partners will keep watch during a heist and not turn on them afterward. In every street transaction, trust—whether implicit or explicit—plays a vital role. Without it, the game collapses and becomes impossible.

If someone truly adhered to the "trust no one" mantra, they would have no choice but to isolate themselves completely, removing all opportunity for betrayal or harm and leaving street life altogether.

But street life, and life in general, doesn't allow for such isolation. People may be reluctant to trust, but at some point, they must entrust others with their lives, their secrets, or their livelihood. Every relationship, no matter how transactional, carries some degree of vulnerability—a reality that renders the myth of absolute distrust impossible to sustain.

What this myth truly reflects is not the absence of trust, but its careful negotiation. In street life, trust becomes transactional, conditional, and selective, much like respect. Experience may teach caution, but it also reveals the necessity of trust, even in criminal enterprises. Without trust, paranoia and fear take over, destabilizing even the most calculated operations. This double-edged sword—you're damned if you trust and damned if you don't—creates a cycle of mistrust that feeds into the very trauma that perpetuates the myth.

At its core, the mantra "trust no one" is a reflection of trauma. For many, it stems from repeated betrayals, childhood neglect, police brutality, or toxic relationships. In street life and households across every class on the spectrum, experiences of broken trust—abuse, abandonment, or deceit—leave deep scars. Trauma becomes a learned behavior, shaping how individuals approach relationships and connections. Worse, this trauma is often passed on to others through what is known as secondary trauma.

Secondary trauma occurs when individuals absorb the fears, biases, and mistrust of those they admire or depend on. A young person who hears "trust no one" from a beloved elder, one of the "big homies," or an entertainer they admire may internalize that fear without fully understanding where it comes from. A child may develop resentment toward a parent when they hear negative words spoken about them by the other. Racism can take root when children are taught to hate people they've never met, solely based on skin color or cultural differences. People may even begin to distrust institutions—like schools, law enforcement, hospitals, or counseling services—not because of their own experience, but because of what others have said about them, causing them to avoid resources that could help.

This emotional hand-me-down becomes a form of inherited trauma—a self-fulfilling prophecy. It spreads like a silent infection, turning people into carriers of wounds that aren't fully theirs. One or two negative experiences can then validate what was transferred emotionally and cause the individual to spiral even faster than the one who originally passed down the trauma, whether quietly, through internal turmoil, or loudly, through rage and outbursts.

Even as the mantra is glorified in music, tattooed on bodies, or repeated in conversations, it reinforces a cycle of harm. While it may sound empowering or wise, it damages the potential for healthy relationships. Those who embrace this mindset close themselves off from meaningful connections, perpetuating the very isolation they seek to avoid.

Ultimately, the myth "trust no one" is less about truth and more about survival mechanisms distorted by pain or confusion. Trust, like vulnerability, is unavoidable. The key is not to avoid it entirely but to navigate it with discernment and intention. As President Ronald Reagan famously put it, "Trust but verify." Without trust, humanity loses its essential glue. The breakdown of trust is the breakdown of connection, and in that void lies loneliness, paranoia, and despair.

> "Abandon weapons first, then food. But never abandon trust. People cannot get on without trust. Trust is more important than life."
> —CONFUCIUS

As important as it is to protect oneself, it is equally crucial to recognize that trust, however risky, is the foundation of every relationship, every interaction, and every act of survival in life—including street life. The myth may feel like armor, but it is, in reality, a chain binding those who truly live by it to a life of fear and isolation.

STREET VIEW

Imagine a criminal telling another criminal, "You can't trust criminals." The irony is sharp, but it perfectly captures the contradictory nature of trust in street life. Throughout my life—before, during, and after my time in the streets—I've experienced every angle of trust. I've trusted too much, trusted too little, and eventually reached a point where I tried to avoid trusting altogether. Over time, I developed serious trust issues. To protect myself, I built walls, created distance, and guarded against anyone or anything that might make me let my guard down.

At first, the bubble I created felt safe. I convinced myself that isolation from others would keep me from being hurt or betrayed again and again. But over time, the isolation turned lonely. Legitimate opportunities began slipping away as I questioned people's intentions and motives, driven by my own paranoia. My inability to trust left me unbalanced, unable to discern who or what was good for me. I became stuck, playing into the myth of "trust no one," even though, deep down, I knew that my trust issues—while reasonable and, in most cases, explainable—were far from helpful.

Eventually, I started peeling back the layers of my distrust. I realized my struggles with trust began long before street life. I was first exposed to pain and disappointment in my childhood, with no one to guide me through it. To make matters worse, that pain came from the people I was conditioned to love and trust the most—social structures and family. The abandonment, betrayal, and misdirection I experienced left a deep scar.

In my search for belonging, I turned to the streets—a place just as broken and unbalanced as I was. When someone who's already broken enters a broken system, the result is shattering. Yet, in my desire for camaraderie and the family I didn't have, I freely gave my trust. I kept it 100, assuming others would do the same. Instead, I was betrayed, manipulated, and left to face harsh consequences for my loyalty. Each betrayal—the robberies, attempted robberies, and attempted murders on my life, and later being snitched out—reinforced the myth that I couldn't trust anyone. Everyone was now suspect.

I sat in prison cells replaying those betrayals and many more, inside and outside of street life, dissecting the motives behind them, and remembering how those I never forgot seemed to forget me. My bubble of isolation felt justified, but I couldn't ignore the truth: I missed trusting people. I missed the feeling of connection, of taking a leap of faith, even if it came with risks. I missed the innocence of trust, no matter how dangerous it was.

Through reflection, I learned a hard truth: it's better to trust and be proven wrong than to never trust and never know. Yes, trusting comes with risks—sometimes great losses and indescribable pain—but life itself is trial and error. Trust is the foundation of growth, connection, and forward movement.

Without it, I invited stagnation, isolation, and self-inflicted failures.

I soon learned that the myth "trust no one" masquerades as strength, but in reality, it's a delusion. If we can't find a way to trust, that's a clear sign we're in the wrong situation. We must either redirect ourselves or risk losing far more. While trust may leave us vulnerable, it is also what propels us forward, builds relationships, and creates opportunities, as I found out through my own experiences. To live without trust is not protection—it's self-destruction. The self-destruction may not come all at once, but it will come, little by little.

Trust is strongest—and most meaningful—when it serves the collective good of humanity, not just the interests of a select few.

THE TRUTH

Trust is a perilous game that we are all forced to play, and no path in life will guarantee fairness among the players. Those who pretend to live without it are delusional or maybe even outright liars. Trust is essential to success, including our own existence. It is a community that builds for survival and collectively stays prepared for the unknown or the unexpected. And if we can't trust someone or the community, then clearly we must find a way to remove ourselves from both entirely.

TRUST, BUT BE CAREFUL.

MYTH 20

THERE ARE NO WAYS OUT OF STREET LIFE

> Street life is a one-way road with no exits. Once you in, you in fo life. You bound by the rules, the reputation, and everything that comes with it. The streets don't forgive or forget. To walk away is betrayal. Trying to leave yo homies ain't cool.

Street life is often seen as a one-way road to destruction, with no visible exits. Some who glance at it and many more who immerse themselves in this world frequently accept this as truth, envisioning premature death, sometimes before reaching the age of eighteen, as an inevitability. For others, the street's lure lies in the perceived security it offers—a sense of belonging built on fear, loyalty, and promises of relentless dedication to its supposed code. Breaking away feels impossible, as the streets demand not just participation but submission.

Quietly, however, many are suffocated by the weight of this loyalty. They cling to the belief that leaving the streets means losing everything, especially the friendships and connections they think they've solidified. Yet loyalty can become a danger. While it can foster trust, security, and camaraderie, it can also hinder personal growth. Blind or one-sided loyalty has a tendency to trap individuals in unhealthy cycles, leaving them vulnerable to exploitation, emotional burdens like anxiety and low self-esteem, and inner conflict that clouds decision-making. True loyalty should encourage growth, stability, and reciprocity, not stifle potential or create self-destructive patterns. Phrases like "death before dishonor," "my A1 since day one," and "till the wheels fall off" often sound prematurely binding, as no one can truly predict another's intentions over time.

The myth that "there are no ways out of street life" is ultimately self-defeating. It's akin to a pilot deliberately crashing a plane, believing there's no runway in sight, without ever daring to attempt the unthinkable—landing in the harshest terrain under impossible conditions. What feels impossible only remains that way until someone proves otherwise. As Chesley B. Sullenberger—famously known as Sully, the pilot who safely landed a jet on the Hudson River—once pointed out, nothing is possible until someone does it for the first time. His example, like that of many others, shows that even when exits seem nonexistent, the courage to try can redefine what's possible.

Still, this myth endures, perpetuated by those who affirm its narrative. That's not to say that finding a way out is easy. For some, their entrenchment in the streets is so deep that an attempt to leave could cost them everything, including their lives. But even so, the last action we take—our final attempt—might also be our best.

Any lifestyle that offers a sense of comfort, identity, and the illusion of freedom and its unlimited opportunities is difficult to leave behind. Street life becomes an addiction, an anchor of complacency that is not often recognized. Personal relationships and family ties often intertwine with street culture, complicating any effort to walk away. This creates a symbiotic bond that makes every potential exit harder to navigate. Even Elijah Anderson, in *Code of the Street*, observed that even families striving to live by "decent" values often feel compelled to expose their children to the street code, if only to help them navigate and survive the realities of inner-city life.

It's important to note that not all affiliates of street life feel trapped. Many embrace their lifestyle with pride: regardless of potential risks and outcomes, or even the possibility of a peaceful, bright exit, they have no desire to change. But for those who long for an escape, the belief in "no way out" becomes a lonely battle. Like the kind of solitude that often surrounds individuals with higher standards or deeper ambitions, this loneliness can feel isolating—but it also speaks to the unique potential to envision and build something different. As photographer Yousuf Karsh once observed, such isolation can be both the cost and the catalyst of creation.

Still, potential alone isn't enough. The emotional weight of isolation is heavy, especially when the road out is long and uncertain.

The words of encouragement people leaving the streets need rarely come from the voices they most want to hear. Breaking free requires not just an open door but the will to step through, even in the absence of reassurance.

Leaving the streets isn't glamorous for most, and it isn't easy. For some, it can be lonely and quiet as many old friends may fall off, never to be heard from again, while new friendships take time to build, as all good things do. The rush of danger is gone, replaced with boredom, loneliness, and routine. But those moments of silence are humbling. Like a baby in the womb, that's where new life begins.

STREET VIEW

When something in life becomes central to our identity, it shapes everything—our decisions, perceptions, and emotional compass. It can give us purpose, but it can also distort our understanding of ourselves and the world around us. Accepting the myth that "there are no ways out of street life" is like putting blinders on—it narrows our vision and traps us in a mindset that keeps us running in circles. When I believed this myth, I unknowingly sentenced myself to a life that felt inescapable, not because the doors weren't there but because years of self- and societal conditioning had convinced me they didn't exist—at least not for me.

This belief didn't just dim my hope; it redefined how I saw myself and others. I started to lose faith in my ability, and at times desire, to change. I started to lose confidence in everyone, and even in the idea of a better world. The myth became like outdated software that I couldn't upgrade, locking me into a system of thinking where loyalty to the streets was everything, and stepping away seemed like betrayal. I thought I knew it all because I was forced to learn life on my own, and because of that, I became too smart for my own good. My knowledge of things would not take a backseat to outside views and possibilities. I told myself that the streets were my family and my homies couldn't survive without me. I thought my presence was central to their survival as I foolishly assumed that I couldn't survive without them. That belief gave me a sense of purpose, a position of pride, of being 100. Real. But it also blinded me to the fact that I was sacrificing my own growth for an illusion of loyalty and a distortion of reality.

Since my childhood, the streets had seduced me like candy from a stranger—offering what seemed sweet but hid certain dangers I couldn't see at first. Even as a child, I faced the consequences of being lured into "the life." Over time, I developed not just a connection to the streets but an emotional and psychological dedication to the lifestyle. It was like Stockholm syndrome; I felt bonded to something that was ultimately harming me. Even as I grew older and started to see the cracks in the illusion, walking away felt impossible. I realized that not everyone in the streets was as committed as I was, nor were they living the life for the same reasons, but the thought of leaving still felt like betrayal—of the streets, my homies, and even myself. I took to heart the saying "your word is all you have" and applied it not only to others, but ultimately to myself.

Keeping my word had become a cornerstone of my character, loyalty was my religion, and being solid became who I was—and all of those things gave me pride. I was a part of something that felt exclusive, like a club that rejected the larger system, which had already rejected me. As the old ancient proverb says, "The enemy of my enemy is my friend." This made me feel important. The streets gave me purpose, a place to test my strengths, face my fears, and prove myself. It provided opportunities—though they were often dangerous—and gave me a sense of belonging, even the illusion of safety. I believed I was giving back to the streets as much as I assumed it was giving me, not realizing that the streets don't give you anything; you have to earn, negotiate, or take. Everything I took, earned, or negotiated demanded much more in return.

Prior to leaving, I believed the streets were all I had. Considering my mindset at that time, they very well could have been. This is why the myth of "there are no ways out of street life" resonates so deeply. For me, the streets felt like the only place where I was seen, valued, or even alive. The streets offer a sense of survival and the idea of brotherhood, but they also offer fear of what's on the outside. When you've been rejected by family or even society—whether through racism, poverty, betrayal, or incarceration—the streets become both a refuge and a prison.

But the truth is that there are ways out. They're rarely glamorous, rarely ideal, and almost never what we imagine, but they exist. The problem is that we often wait for the "perfect" option—a flawless opportunity to finally walk away from the streets. I used to tell myself the right time would come when I'd have enough money, when the pieces would fall neatly into place on my terms. But there are no perfect options. Every option is just a step forward, a chance to move toward something new. And every step, no matter how small, is still an option.

The real challenge wasn't money. When I finally had it, I still didn't leave. What held me back ran deeper: fear of leaving the homies, bitterness toward society, and my own insecurities. I had to face the thought of being the "new guy" in a world I didn't understand, being second-rate, maybe even being treated like shit in a place I didn't care for anyway. It felt like switching to a new school—leaving old friends behind, already hating the system, and being embarrassed at having to start from scratch.

Leaving the streets isn't about finding a perfect path; for me it was about choosing to walk a different one, even if it felt uncertain. Each option is an opportunity, not an endpoint. It's a way to begin a lifelong journey toward experiences that are healthier, calmer, and more fulfilling. And the truth is, the streets, as an entity, don't care if you stay loyal or walk away—

because they just keep moving with or without you and will forever have people who are willing to replace you as soon as you leave.

To escape the grip of the myth, I had to recognize that growth often requires discomfort, and even a lot of boredom. It means facing fears, doubts, and the guilt of leaving something that once felt like home. But it also means embracing the unknown and trusting that there's more to life than the streets. Like moving out of your parents' home or getting your first apartment, it can be scary sleeping in a strange place all alone, but you know there's no turning back. The streets may offer survival, but they don't offer or give every type of fulfillment. That's something I had to discover on my own, one imperfect and sometimes lonely step at a time.

THE TRUTH

Despite the obstacles, emotional entrapments, and harmful narrative that street life is inescapable, exits and paths do exist, even if they're difficult to see or achieve. Life is paved with struggles and challenges, and escaping street life is part of that reality. The roads are shaky and can feel like they are crumbling under your feet. Nevertheless, it is a journey that awaits those who want more than they have been raised with or have been conditioned to assume there's nothing else.

THERE'S ALWAYS A WAY OUT.

MYTH 21

FELONS CAN'T MAKE IT IN SOCIETY

> The world doesn't forgive felons. Once you're branded, society sees you as nothing more than a criminal. Employers won't hire you, landlords won't rent to you, and people won't trust you. The opportunities others take for granted are off-limits to someone with a record. The system is built to make you fail—it sets you up to come back to the streets so it can put you back in prison. Making it in society as a felon isn't just hard; it's pretty much impossible.

The belief that felons can't make it in society is a myth deeply ingrained in both individual and collective minds. It is a narrative shaped by prejudice, systemic barriers, and fear, but its greatest power lies in how it discourages felons from believing in their own potential. Despite being disproved by countless success stories, the myth persists, feeding a vicious cycle of defeat and reinforcing the very obstacles it claims are insurmountable.

This myth operates like a psychological virus. It spreads through environments steeped in doubt and despair, amplified by slogans like "fuck school" or "ain't no future for us." These messages, often repeated casually in conversation, in music, and in street culture, become self-fulfilling prophecies. They strip away hope and desire, convincing individuals that failure in any new direction is inevitable. As Hill Harper has observed, one of the hardest challenges for anyone with a felony is breaking the cycle of recidivism. His words bear truth—but they touch only one part of the myth's reach. The myth does more than target individuals; it infiltrates entire communities, cementing the belief that life beyond the streets is not only unattainable but irrelevant.

This toxic mindset becomes a weapon wielded to crush ambition. When felons hear phrases like "once a felon, always a felon" or "the system will always be against you," these words don't just state perceived facts; they can start to shape identity. They maintain mental chains long after the physical ones have been removed. This weaponization of doubt encourages stagnation, making the idea of change seem both impossible and undesirable. It reinforces the street slogan "stay in yo lane," meaning they should stay where they are, in familiar territory, rather than risking the pain and humiliation of rejection in a society that often does little to welcome them in or welcome them back.

However, this narrative is dangerously misleading. While it's true that systemic barriers—employment discrimination, housing restrictions, and public stigma—exist, these challenges, though real, are not insurmountable. The system's flaws, combined with societal reluctance to fully embrace rehabilitation, certainly make reintegration or integration difficult. There are draconian laws, disgusted people, and institutions designed to hinder rather than help felons, yet these despicable obstacles do not make success totally impossible.

In fact, many felons overcome these barriers, often with remarkable resilience. Some go on to lead in business, like Larry Miller, who served time for murder as a teen before becoming a top Nike executive. Others find their voice in the arts, such as Charles S. Dutton, Mark Wahlberg, Tim Allen, David Crosby, Danny Trejo, and Christian Slater, many of whom served jail or prison sentences before building successful acting or music careers. Literature has its own examples: Donald Goines, Chester Himes, Piper Kerman, Jack Abbott, and Jeff Henderson all turned incarceration into storytelling that reached millions. Even in the face of long odds, women like Cyntoia Brown Long and Debbie Peagler transformed personal tragedy into powerful advocacy. These stories prove that while the journey may be strenuous, it is far from hopeless. Felons can and do succeed—and for every person with a well-known story, there are countless others quietly living thriving and fulfilling lives—but the first step is rejecting the myth that a destructive past guarantees a destructive future.

What makes this myth particularly insidious is how it strips away the courage to try. For many felons, the climb back into society feels as painful as the fall into incarceration. Fear of failure, judgment, or humiliation often leads to paralysis. Psychological struggles, such as depression, anxiety, or unresolved trauma, add to the weight, making even small steps feel impossible. This paralysis is compounded by the myth's external influences, which whisper that it's safer to stay in familiar darkness than risk rejection in the pursuit of brighter opportunities.

The transition from street life to mainstream society presents unique challenges. Street life often provides a sense of belonging and identity, however flawed or dangerous it may be. It offers an environment where aggression, power, and survival are open and understood currencies. In many ways, it becomes a world of opportunity for those seeking a different kind of life—one built not on legality or stability, but on immediacy, grit, and reputation. In some cases, for those looking to use street life as a means to an end, it offers that "one extra push."

Ironically, this raw pursuit of a better life echoes the ideals America once promised to the world. The Statue of Liberty, long regarded as a beacon of hope and reinvention, stands as a symbol of refuge for the lost and overlooked—words etched into its foundation declare a welcome to the tired, the poor, and the rejected, not unlike those coming from the streets seeking another way.

> "Give me your tired, your poor, your huddled masses yearning to breathe free. The wretched refuse of your teeming shore. Send these, the homeless, the tempest-tossed to me, I lift my lamp beside the golden door!"
>
> —EMMA LAZARUS, "THE NEW COLOSSUS" (1883)

Society, by contrast, claims to be lawful and civil, yet often greets felons with unspoken aggression, prejudice, racism, and unchecked hostility. This hypocrisy and street-like behavior become a trigger for many felons, who are conditioned—in most cases since childhood—to respond to aggression with aggression. In moments of misunderstanding or frustration, years of progress can be undone in seconds for some felons. As Jadakiss, one of hip-hop's most respected voices, has pointed out, letting personal feelings interfere with the work at hand will only come back to hurt you in the long run. While he may have stated this principle in a general sense, it applies just as much to individuals with records as it does to the systems around them—employers, officers, judges, and even neighbors. For felons especially, when emotions cloud judgment, second chances get buried under stereotypes.

This, however, is where the myth must be challenged most directly. The streets do not have to be the end of the road, nor does a criminal record have to define someone's worth or future. Felons who break free from the grip of this myth do more than reclaim their own lives; they rewrite the narrative for future generations. By confronting fear and unlearning the doubts instilled by their environments, misdirected upbringings, or societal prejudices, they pave the way for others to follow.

It's not an easy road, and setbacks are inevitable. But the fact remains: felons can succeed. The process begins with unlearning the poison of defeatism. For every slogan like "fuck school," there must be a louder voice saying "fuck it—go to school." For every dismissal of ambition, there must be reminders that change is not only possible but necessary. Everything changes in life. No form of success is guaranteed, and some may be impossible, but many others are achievable. It starts with rejecting the myth that failure is inevitable. Rapper and activist Nipsey Hussle defied these stereotypes and built legitimate businesses inside his own community. That quiet act of self-betterment, done outside the spotlight, challenged the stereotype of what street-affiliated men are "supposed" to be. He didn't abandon the streets to seek knowledge—he expanded who he was beyond them.

Felons can learn society, just as they learned a life of crime. Both environments require guidance, trust, and adaptability. Crossing into society is like stepping into a new neighborhood: unfamiliar at first but navigable with the right support. As they step onto this path, felons must remember that there's no shame in seeking help and that being "second best" at times challenges ambition, just as street life did.

Whether in education, mentorship, or advocacy, no one succeeds alone. The myth persists because it thrives on isolation and fear, but by embracing connection and resilience, felons can move beyond it. Sometimes the most transformative step is simply reaching out. As actress and advocate Vanessa Williams once emphasized, you never know where help might come from unless you're willing to ask. Facing obstacles doesn't mean facing them alone, and seeking support can open doors you didn't know existed.

Ultimately, the myth that felons can't make it in society is a lie told to keep individuals and communities trapped. Felons who rise above it don't just succeed; they prove that their futures are theirs to define. The climb is hard, but it is worth it. And for those willing to take that leap, many parts of society offer not just a challenge but a chance to redefine what success really means.

"Go off and try new things, especially if it's going to help you become a better person and more educated in life. Because in 10 years, most of the same niggas will still be in the streets on the same corners, doing the same shit. If you don't make it in the new things you try, I promise you, that the streets will still be here for you so you can continue to be a street nigga if that's what you want. Never forget. Life is all about growth and development."

—RICKY G

STREET VIEW

Throughout my time in street life, I've seen many fail at their "reentry" into society. I can honestly say I was one of those failures—though I wasn't "reentering," but entering for the first time. I carried multiple felonies, had made many trips in and out of LA County Jail, even caught a case in Illinois, and did two prison terms—one federal and one state. No matter how I got there and regardless of the lack of guidance from my upbringing and all the trauma I had experienced, the responsibility was never on society, and it clearly had never been on my parents. From the day I was born, it seemed to have always been on me—even as a child without anyone to guide me toward knowledge or to help me understand the dangers and the abuse I was subjected to. That is the purpose of a society, but it was on me before I even knew it was, forced to be an adult before I was a teen. Learn to break that cycle or stop it before it begins.

As a boy, I was abandoned to the streets and conditioned to believe in its myths. Family was just a term; you're either lucky enough to be born with supportive parents or you're not. So early on, the streets felt like a place that understood my anger and my loneliness and offered assistance to help me cope and get out of the mental, physical, and financial poverty I was experiencing while relieving me of being the burden I thought I was on every adult in my life.

In street life, I was abused in many different ways by law enforcement. Those who swore to protect and serve the public physically beat me on countless occasions, and even at the age of sixteen, I was detained on the streets by the Chicago PD and threatened that I'd be taken somewhere and stripped if I did not unzip my pants and lift my balls, right there, to prove that I wasn't hiding crack cocaine under them. I hadn't started selling cocaine or crack at the time. Still, I already knew how unlawful law enforcement really was—based upon my experiences in California with the Los Angeles County Sheriff's Department, Bell Gardens PD, Long Beach PD, Compton PD, and others—and how much more monstrous they could become, so I felt it was better to take the assault and comply. It was apparent to me that law enforcement was designed to be what it was everywhere, reinforcing the hypocrisy, the mask society wears.

Given that, street myths felt more powerful, almost unbreakable; how could I believe in a system where the ones in power were no better than those who despised me for the neighborhood I was from, the gang colors I wore, or which way a hat was worn on my head? The lines between right and wrong blurred and became questionable, and I bought into the myths even more, as they felt like the only truths I could hold on to.

So how could I "reenter" society if I had never been a part of it in the first place? How could I rejoin something I was never properly or personally invited into? The innocence of some children is protected, while other children are exposed at a young age to "society's" authoritarianism, racism, classism, favoritism, pessimism, and sexism. Many of us became a burden, society's shame and premature failure, and later became its felons.

It felt like society decided my place long before I had a say. Some of us turned to the streets in hopes of changing the narrative, no matter how dismal it may have seemed. This is what happens when people desperately need to find a way to make it in life or even belong.

I, like many others, was blamed for my position, as if I was hustling for my wants—like name-brand shoes and the latest outfits—and not my needs—like paying bills and finding a desperately needed place to live. Some of us were forced to make adult decisions as the journey from elementary school to prison yards became inevitable. My release from prison wasn't about reentering society; it was about figuring out how to enter society for the first time.

With all the embedded scars, childhood trauma, upbringing and conditioning, heavy weight of skepticism, and now a criminal record, I needed more from the system than the one-size-fits-all approach.

For many of us felons, there was no family support, no resourceful community, no financial assistance, no therapeutic sessions, and no history of ever having employment, so the "reentry" programs that assume a second chance only scratch the surface, addressing the obvious issues but not the deeper ones.

But, of course, some felons or street affiliates are comfortable in their reality and have no intention of changing, no desire to enter or reenter society—I was once one of them. Others, meanwhile, struggle to shake the addiction of street life, as it becomes normalized along with all the myths. Without resources and meaningful connections, many will constantly fail under their own weight as society comfortably prejudges and dissolves all resources and opportunities.

Despite it all—and for all of us—there is life after street life.

There is hope in places we may have never looked, a brighter destiny we may be ignoring. The past doesn't have to define us, and the present doesn't have to trap us. Inner wounds and outer obstacles can fall behind if we dare to walk forward.

For me, that meant trying new things—no matter how unfamiliar they felt or how uncomfortable they made me. I refused to let my experiences go to waste. I told my story, just as I hope you'll one day tell yours.

I found more as I tried more. I grew in character by seizing opportunities, exploring new places, and patiently adjusting to unfamiliar worlds—just as I had once learned the streets. I endured its hardships, ran its obstacles, and whether I won or lost, I didn't fold. I withstood the pressure even when it was crushing me.

I became slow to speak and quick to listen. I began doing things I never imagined: writing books, opening a business, shifting my mindset, practicing patience, and even enduring boredom and trusting the slow process of change.

I started challenging my old beliefs—the ones that had once made me feel secure—and stopped treating my assumptions like facts. I learned that not all criticism is meant to harm me, that my insecurities are my greatest threat, and that I am often my own worst enemy.

I accepted help. I learned to ask for it. I appreciated what little I had. And I fought the stigma that I was nothing more than a felon.

There's hope beyond the twenty-one myths. There's hope in this book. There's hope in my story—and I hope that we all can find hope in places that seem not to have any.

No matter how dismal, how broken, or how far gone things may seem, find the opportunity. Home in on the possibility. And use your ambition.

THE TRUTH

There are no guarantees in life, but a felon's path to success is not impossible as the myth suggests. With access to affordable resources, healthy support, and a commitment to change, a felon can evolve into someone entirely different from their past self. Success begins with an open mind, fueled by ambition and a willingness to explore the many legal opportunities available. Though the road may be steeper and the obstacles more numerous, a felon who is prepared to navigate these challenges has a greater chance of thriving in society. Transformation is not just possible—it's attainable for those ready to put in the work and embrace a new way of life.

FELONS CAN SUCCEED—CHANGE AND OPPORTUNITY MAKE IT POSSIBLE.

CONCLUSION

In peeling back the layers of these twenty-one myths, we've exposed the sharp divide between fact and fiction, perception and reality. The analyses, Street Views, and words from the famous—past and present—remind us that street life is far from simple and its myths are anything but harmless. These myths shape decisions, fuel ambitions, and in most cases, lead to destruction. By confronting them, we don't just dismantle falsehoods; we uncover the humanity, pain, and resilience beneath them. The truth is always more complicated than the myth, and only by looking below the surface can we begin to understand the streets, the people who walk them, and the lives forever shaped by these illusions.

Let these insights stand as a testament to the real experiences behind the myths—a call for deeper understanding and, perhaps, the possibility of change. While this book focuses on street life, its themes resonate far beyond the urban landscape. The myths of street life mirror those found in other cultures, societies, and even institutions. No nation, race, or mind is immune. As we've seen, even the so-called righteous—politicians, community leaders, socialites, religious fanatics, and everyday citizens—drift between civility and crime, glorifying and vilifying the streets in the same breath, romanticizing the image, the culture, the destruction, the ambition, and definitely the characters, past and present.

Street culture is deeply woven into the fabric of society; it has shaped many families of all races, classes, and backgrounds, pushing them to build identities through criminality, gang life, greed, or moral corruption. The rawness of trap houses and the normalization of aggressive mentalities have become so familiar that even mothers and grandmothers can be heard bragging about their street history, mindsets, and affiliations—proof that street life respects no boundaries of age or gender.

Many are drawn to its intensity, and the myths surrounding it stand as testaments to its power. Myths, by their nature, can uplift or destroy, inspire hope or lead us down treacherous paths. The world itself—through religions, governments, and traditions—is shrouded in myths, and street culture is no exception. Myths are tools, often wielded to justify actions or maintain control. When injected into entertainment—music with hypnotic beats, movies with powerful actors, television with sensational storylines—they become seductive, mesmerizing, and dangerously realistic. Applied blindly to life, they sow regret, whether in this generation or the next.

The twenty-one myths of street life should have been examined long before now. But myths in the "right" or "wrong" hands are lucrative: they entertain, generate power, perpetuate legacies, and multiply followers. They hypnotize the young and give purpose to the old. As a result, they've been ignored, propped up, and expanded to serve various and destructive agendas. And when those who lived the life wake up and speak against the myths, their words rarely echo with the same force that their earlier words once hyped crowds. They aren't elevated beyond their past, so the myths go on as gospel, resurrected again and again, while the new message is buried deeper with each generation.

Are there more myths to be told? Undoubtedly. Could we have dug deeper? Perhaps. Did we tread carefully to avoid repetition and overlap? Absolutely. Can my words be challenged? Probably. But this is not the final word on the subject—it is a foundation, a spark to ignite further exploration, insight, and intellectual uplifting. Yet reflection alone isn't enough—the reality is that the myths are alive, breathing, and persistent.

As long as human ambition exists, and as long as cities, towns, and neighborhoods are connected by highways, roads, and blocks, street life will endure. It will persist in urban alleys, rural backroads, and every space in between—because wherever people are excluded, pushed into corners, or fueled by myths that stoke their desires, they will congregate, strategize, and act. Whether on land, at sea, or in the air, the drive to move within or outside manmade laws will continue.

The question remains: What do we do with this understanding? Do we reevaluate our values or accept the streets and their myths as nothing more than inevitable human behavior? Do we challenge what we think we know, along with all we have been taught? Do we dare to question our most cherished beliefs, even if the truth is discomforting? Do we sacrifice our luxuries for a unified path, or do we stay rooted in the comfort of individualism or territoriality? These are not questions with easy answers—but they are questions worth asking.

Stanley "Tookie" Williams, co-founder of the Crips, once reflected in his book *Blue Rage, Black Redemption* that by refusing to live like a predator, he had uncovered his humanity and taught himself to think critically. His journey from violence to self-education is a reminder that transformation is possible, in or out of street life, but only for those willing to confront their own myths. In his words and in his life, we see that rejecting the role the streets assign can open the door to a truer, more deliberate self.

The myths we've examined here are not just stories—they are signposts, warnings, and, at times, reflections of ourselves. They dare us to look inward, to challenge not only the myths given to us early in life, but also the ones we've subconsciously created for ourselves—and perhaps most importantly, the ones we've unconsciously and dangerously passed on to others.

The question becomes, will we continue to live by illusions or finally confront them for what they are? Do we need the myths, like fairy tales or Santa Claus? Are we afraid to sleep with the lights off, no longer allowing the myths of street life to rock us to sleep or the myths that shroud history to tell us what is true?

In the end, the myths of street life are not only about the streets. They are about humanity—its hunger for power, its capacity for deception, and its potential for transformation. To see the myths clearly is to see ourselves clearly. Yes, that can be unpleasant, but it demands that we look at ourselves, unmasked.

Once you see, you cannot unsee.

Once you learn, you cannot unlearn.

The choice then becomes yours: repeat the myths or rewrite them.

www.ingramcontent.com/pod-product-compliance
Lightning Source LLC
LaVergne TN
LVHW041958060526
838200LV00019B/382/J